ZAG

THE NUMBER-ONE STRATEGY OF HIGH-PERFORMANCE BRANDS

A WHITEBOARD OVERVIEW BY **MARTY NEUMEIER**

ZAG

THE NUMBER-ONE STRATEGY OF HIGH-PERFORMANCE BRANDS

A WHITEBOARD OVERVIEW BY MARTY NEUMEIER

COPYRIGHT © 2007 BY MARTY NEUMEIER

NEW RIDERS IS AN IMPRINT OF PEACHPIT PRESS, A DIVISION OF PEARSON EDUCATION

FIND US ON THE WEB AT: WWW.NEWRIDERS.COM
TO REPORT ERRORS, PLEASE SEND A NOTE TO ERRATA@PEACHPIT.COM

NEW RIDERS IS AN IMPRINT OF PEACHPIT, A DIVISION OF PEARSON EDUCATION

ACQUISITIONS EDITOR: MICHAEL J. NOLAN

PRODUCTION EDITOR: DAVID VAN NESS

BOOK DESIGNER: HEATHER MCDONALD

INDEXER: REBECCA PLUNKETT

PROOFREADER: HAIG MACGREGOR

NOTICE OF RIGHTS
ALL RIGHTS RESERVED. NO PART OF THIS BOOK MAY BE REPRODUCED OR TRANSMITTED IN ANY FORM BY ANY MEANS, ELECTRONIC, MECHANICAL, PHOTOCOPYING, RECORDING, OR OTHERWISE, WITHOUT THE PRIOR WRITTEN PERMISSION OF THE PUBLISHER. FOR INFORMATION ON GETTING PERMISSION FOR REPRINTS AND EXCERPTS, CONTACT PERMISSIONS@PEACHPIT.COM.

NOTICE OF LIABILITY
THE INFORMATION IN THIS BOOK IS DISTRIBUTED ON AN "AS IS" BASIS WITHOUT WARRANTY. WHILE EVERY PRECAUTION HAS BEEN TAKEN IN THE PREPARATION OF THE BOOK, NEITHER THE AUTHOR NOR PEACHPIT SHALL HAVE ANY LIABILITY TO ANY PERSON OR ENTITY WITH RESPECT TO ANY LOSS OR DAMAGE CAUSED OR ALLEGED TO BE CAUSED DIRECTLY OR INDIRECTLY BY THE INSTRUCTIONS CONTAINED IN THIS BOOK OR BY THE COMPUTER SOFTWARE AND HARDWARE PRODUCTS DESCRIBED IN IT.

TRADEMARKS
MANY OF THE DESIGNATIONS USED BY MANUFACTURERS AND SELLERS TO DISTINGUISH THEIR PRODUCTS ARE CLAIMED AS TRADEMARKS. WHERE THOSE DESIGNATIONS APPEAR IN THIS BOOK, AND PEACHPIT WAS AWARE OF A TRADEMARK CLAIM, THE DESIGNATIONS APPEAR AS REQUESTED BY THE OWNER OF THE TRADEMARK. ALL OTHER PRODUCT NAMES AND SERVICES IDENTIFIED THROUGHOUT THIS BOOK ARE USED IN EDITORIAL FASHION ONLY AND FOR THE BENEFIT OF SUCH COMPANIES WITH NO INTENTION OF INFRINGEMENT OF THE TRADEMARK. NO SUCH USE, OR THE USE OF ANY TRADE NAME, IS INTENDED TO CONVEY ENDORSEMENT OR OTHER AFFILIATION WITH THIS BOOK.

ISBN 0-321-42677-0

9 8

NEW RIDERS
1249 EIGHTH STREET, BERKELEY, CA 94710 510/524-2178 800/283-9444 510/524-2221 (FAX)

PRINTED AND BOUND IN THE UNITED STATES OF AMERICA

TO MOM AND DAD, MY BOOKENDS

PREFACE

As the pace of business quickens and the number of brands multiplies, it's customers, not companies, who decide which brands live and which ones die. An overabundance of look-alike products and me-too services is forcing customers to search for something, anything, to help them separate the winners from the clutter.

The solution? When everybody zigs, zag.

You'll find this book a living example of the zag discipline. While many authors start with an article's worth of ideas and expand them to book length, I've taken a book's worth of ideas and compressed them to article length. Instead of a theorist's view from the outside, I've given you a practitioner's view from the inside. Instead of 500 pages of heavy-going case studies, I've squeezed my thoughts into less than 200 pages of easy-to-read, easy-to-use, and easy-to-remember principles. In short, with ZAG, I preach what I practice.

I know your time is valuable, so my first goal is to give you a book you can read on a brief plane ride. My second and more important goal is to give you the insights, process, and courage to build a high-performance brand.

—Marty Neumeier

CONTENTS

BUSINESS HAS ONLY TWO BASIC FUNCTIONS:
MARKETING AND INNOVATION.
—PETER DRUCKER

INTRODUCTION

THE BIG SPEEDUP.

The starter's pistol was fired in 1965 with Gordon Moore's bold prediction: The number of transistors in a given space would double each year, while the cost of each transistor would decrease, and its speed would increase. Forty years later the spirit of Moore's Law still holds, and his company, Intel, remains at the heart of a revolution in speed that has altered our lives in ways we've yet to fully comprehend.

As computing power has grown, so has our access to information. For example, in 1998 Google had an index of 25 million pages. By the end of 2004 its index had grown to 8 billion pages—a 360-fold increase. And the speed? When I entered the search term "speed of business," Google delivered 170 million citations in 0.2 seconds flat.

We now enjoy instant connectivity to our friends and business associates around the world, thanks to cell phones, instant messaging, and e-mail. We're so connected that we risk becoming disconnected. For example, companies have cited "BlackBerrys under the table" as the biggest obstacle to coherent meetings.

We've learned not only to sneak our e-mails during meetings, but to talk on the phone, listen to music, read online documents, and converse with colleagues at the same time. At home we toggle between reading a magazine and listening to music, browsing the Web and watching a football game, cooking a casserole and catching up on world events. News programs no longer consider their offerings rich enough unless they cater to our multitasking habits with a continuous stream of stock quotes, late-breaking news, weather, and other items to activate the edges of our screens.

Manufacturers have a need for speed as well. The winning manufacturer is no longer the one with the best product, but the one with the fastest supply chain. Author and supply-chain expert Rob Rodin explains that companies today have no choice but to connect to the "three insatiable demands of business—free, perfect, and now." Helping make the "now" a reality are broadband computer networks, overnight delivery, RFID tags, and just-in-time processes. Manufacturing leaders such as Dell and Toyota have capitalized on what sociologist Alvin Toffler had predicted in 1965:

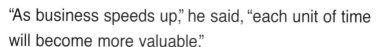

"As business speeds up," he said, "each unit of time will become more valuable."

A century ago a visit to the store might have been an all-day trek, while today most of us can do our shopping right in our neighborhood. In 1986, before the big speed-up, America had more high schools than shopping centers. Today, shopping centers outnumber high schools by two to one. Inside those shopping centers, supermarkets stock more than three times the number of products they did in 1986, and innovations in checkout systems

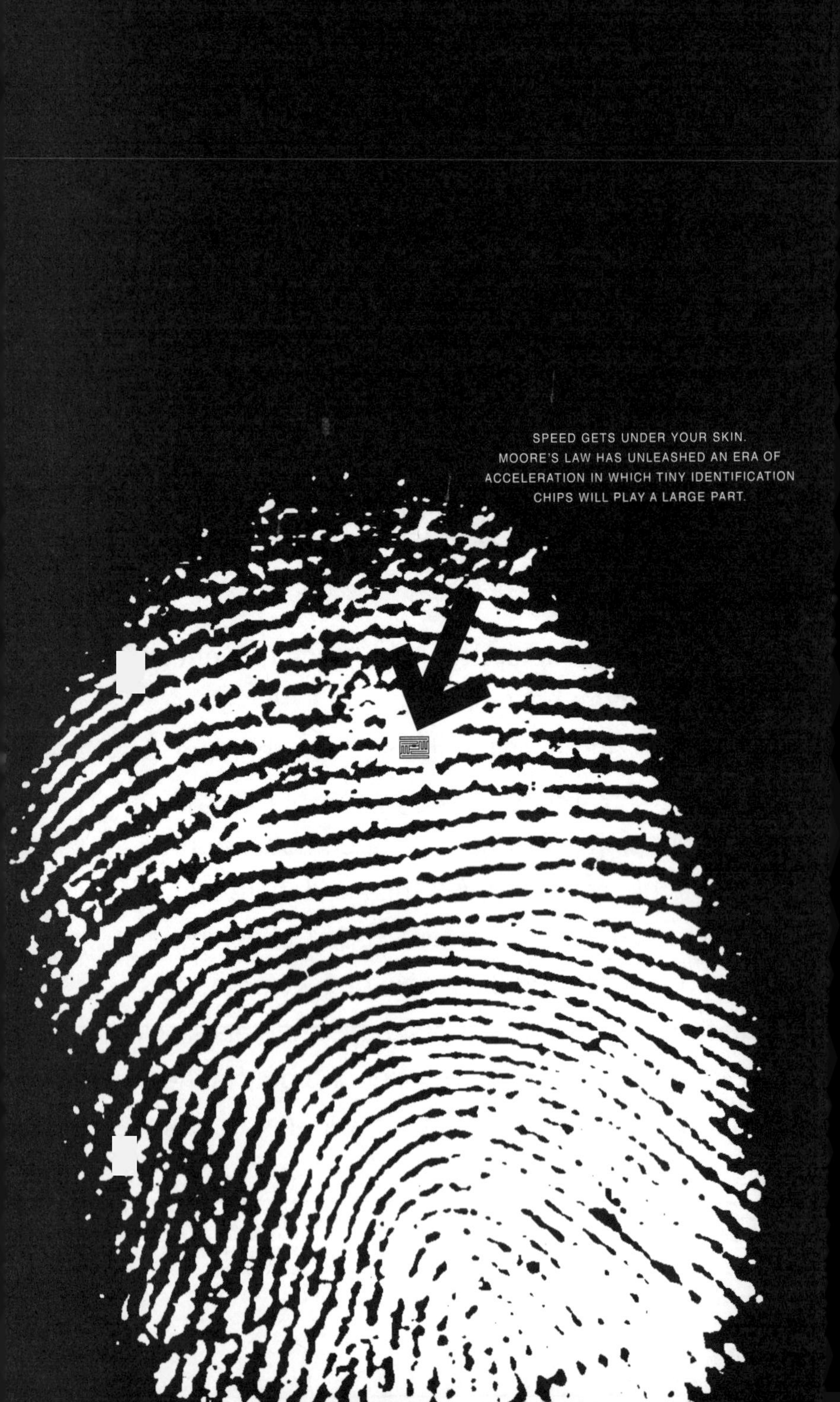
SPEED GETS UNDER YOUR SKIN.
MOORE'S LAW HAS UNLEASHED AN ERA OF
ACCELERATION IN WHICH TINY IDENTIFICATION
CHIPS WILL PLAY A LARGE PART.

are getting customers through the line in less than half the previous time.

Before Moore's Law, Americans were famous non-travelers, with around three million people going to Europe each year. Now, thanks to cheaper fares and a greater choice of airlines and airports, more than 11 million people go to Europe each year. Where do they stay? Possibly at one of the 54,000 hotels listed on Expedia.com. By shopping online they can quickly compare photos, descriptions, and prices, then book their hotels on the spot with a credit card.

Travel is expanding the borders of our eating habits as well. After visiting Europe, for example, we may develop a taste for Belon oysters. A seafood restaurant can then impress us by letting us know that our entree has been flown in fresh from Brittany. The oysters sitting on your plate tonight may have boarded a plane this morning.

McDonald's, the king of fast food, has recently reduced the average meal-delivery time to 121 seconds. They plan to shave off another 15 seconds by adding an RFID check-out system that allows customers to pay without even touching their wallets. Some of us will still be impatient.

THE REAL COMPETITION IS CLUTTER.

We not only live in a world of FASTER, we live in a world of MORE. Traditional marketing strategists tend to frame the competition in terms of other offerings in the same category (i.e., other sports cars). When they think outside the box, they may even include offerings in tangent categories (i.e., sporty sedans and motorcycles). But today's real competition—competition that's so pervasive we can't even see it—doesn't come from direct or even indirect competitors. It comes from the extreme clutter of the marketplace.

When John Wannamaker launched the first department store in 1876, he opened the door to wider customer choice, and our choices have been multiplying ever since. By the time Moore's Law was established in 1965, the average supermarket carried 20,000 items. Now we can choose from among 40,000 items or more. In 2005 alone, 195,000 book titles were published, adding to the four million already in print. In the same year, 40 billion product-jammed catalogs were published in the United States, which amounts to 134 catalogs for every man, woman, and child. In the financial sector, more transactions were recorded in a single day of 2005 than in all of 1965. These are all examples of PRODUCT CLUTTER.

Each product and service is defined by its features, which offers more scope for clutter. We need only compare the features of a 1986 telephone with the features of a 2006 cell phone to see what's possible when engineers put their minds to it. This is an example of FEATURE CLUTTER, which comes from the type of straight-line thinking that says more is always better.

With a growing list of features, companies are naturally more eager to communicate the resulting benefits. This has led to a reported 3,000 marketing messages per day, per person—up from 1,500 at the time of Moore's Law. Yet our ability

MARKETPLACE CLUTTER TAKES 5 FORMS:

1 **PRODUCT CLUTTER**. Too many products and services.

2 **FEATURE CLUTTER**. Too many features in each product.

3 **ADVERTISING CLUTTER**. Too many media messages.

4 **MESSAGE CLUTTER**. Too many elements per message.

5 **MEDIA CLUTTER**. Too many competing channels.

to pay attention to marketing messages hasn't grown at all. The number of messages we can take in, according to The American Association of Advertising Agencies, is still less than 100 per day. Not surprisingly, two-thirds of Americans complain that they feel "constantly bombarded" by ADVERTISING CLUTTER.

If we look more closely at the messages themselves, we may find that the problem gets worse. Research shows that most commercial messages contain too many elements, all competing with one another for our understanding. And the elements themselves may be uninteresting, unclear, or off-message. When CEOs say they know that half of their advertising money is wasted—they just don't know which half—it may be the half that's spent on MESSAGE CLUTTER.

Finally, technology and competition have resulted in MEDIA CLUTTER. In 1960 there were 8,400 magazine titles, 440 radio stations, and 6 television channels. Today there are 12,000 magazine titles, 13,500 radio stations, and 85 television channels, as well as 25,000 Internet broadcast channels that didn't exist before Moore's Law. Back then, television networks competed with other television networks. Today, thanks to our multi-tasking-speed-obsessed culture, they also compete for our time against the computer, the magazine, and the MP3 player.

Despite a 75% increase in advertising, evidence shows we're paying less attention to any given product, service, message, or medium. In an article titled "Complexities of Choice," adwriter Glory Carlberg offered an explanation: "Years ago, the exponents of good merchandising pointed out that in giving a choice you made it more difficult for the prospective buyer to say no. However, it is just possible that today's range of choices may so confuse the buyer that he or she will put up with the old model rather than decide which is the best of the 23 varieties advertised." She wrote that article in 1965.

Ironically, when companies are faced with competition from too many products, services, features, messages, meanings, or media, their first reaction is to fight clutter with more clutter. It's like trying to put out a fire with gasoline.

Esplanade
STAPLES
Circuit City
ULTA
Bally TOTAL FITNESS
THE HOME DEPOT
RIVERPARK
AMC 20
UNION LANDING
ARGET
CENTURY THEATRES
Albertsons Savon
OfficeMax
Michaels
IHOP
chili's
Mancini's SLEEPWORLD
MICRO C
T·J·maxx
BEN & JERRY'S
yoyo sushi
WENDY'S
McDonald's
DRIVE-THRU
OPEN 24 HOURS

LEVITZ
FURNITURE

RAVENSWOOD
Office
DEPOT
76

MOTOR
HARLEY-DAVIDSON
CYCLES

to win a
$100 Macy's
Gift Card

GASOLINE
SELF SERVE
High Performance
289 9/10

GASOLINE
SELF SERVE
Unleaded Plus
269 9/10

COURTYARD
Marriott

Residence
Inn
Marriott

am
pm

IKEA

[AHH, ISN'T THAT BETTER?]

BRAND-TO-BRAND COMBAT.

The human mind deals with clutter the best way it can—by blocking most of it out. What gets in, those items that seem most useful or interesting, are labeled and stored in little mental boxes. Once a label goes on and a box is filled, the mind resists making changes to it. This simple fact has a profound effect on how businesses now compete.

To sustain success, companies have always needed to erect barriers to competition. At the beginning of the industrial revolution, for example, the favored barrier was ownership of the means of production. If a company had a knitting machine and its competitors didn't, the company with the machine usually won.

When most companies had machines, the barrier to competition became the factory. If a company could afford to own and manage a large factory with trained employees and conveyor-belt efficiencies, the company with the factory won.

Later, when many companies had factories, the barrier to competition became access to capital. If a company could raise capital by selling shares or putting its factory up as collateral, the company with the capital won.

As manufacturing began to give way to the information economy, the barrier moved from monetary capital to intellectual capital. If a company had patents and copyrights to keep competitors from reproducing its products and processes, the company with the patents won.

Today, the intellectual capital barrier is showing cracks. Yesterday's patents are losing their value as companies leapfrog each other in a constant race to innovate. Not only that, using intellectual property as a barrier can sometimes hurt companies rather than help them, since it can slow the growth of the business ecosystems that allow them to thrive. An example is Apple Computer's early decision to keep its operating platform closely held while Microsoft's standard platform swept the field.

Now, the battleground is moving again. While intellectual property, access to capital, and manufacturing efficiencies are still important, the newest barriers to competition are the mental walls that customers erect to keep out clutter. For the first time in history, the most powerful barriers to competition are not controlled by companies, but by customers. Those little boxes they build in their minds determine the boundaries of brands.

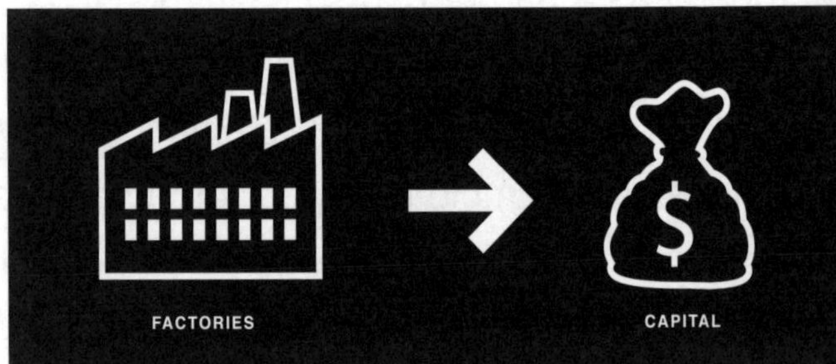
FACTORIES
CAPITAL

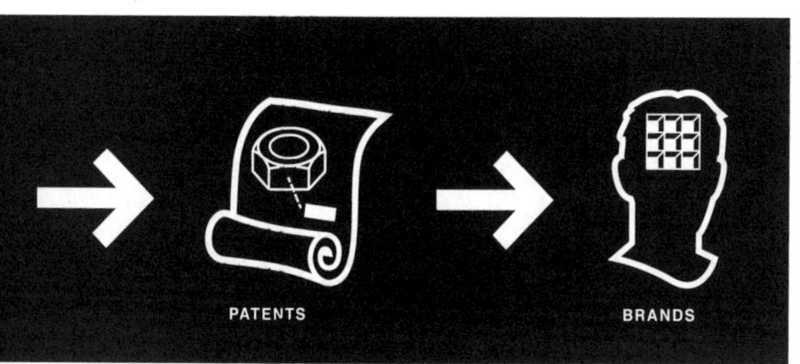

THE BARRIERS
TO COMPETITION
HAVE MOVED FROM
THE PHYSICAL TO
THE INTELLECTUAL,
AND FROM WITHIN THE
COMPANY'S CONTROL
TO OUTSIDE IT.

A **BRAND** IS A PERSON'S GUT FEELING ABOUT A PRODUCT, SERVICE, OR COMPANY.

THE NEW DEFINITION OF BRAND.

What exactly is a brand? Hint: It's not a company's logo or advertising. Those things are controlled by the company. Instead, a brand is a customer's gut feeling about a product, service, or company. People create brands to bring order out of clutter. If the word BRAND didn't exist, we'd have to invent a new one, because no other word captures the complexity and richness of this concept. The only word that comes close is "reputation." Your personal reputation, like a company's brand, lies outside your control. It's not what YOU say it is—it's what THEY say it is. The best you can do is influence it.

If a brand is a customer's gut feeling, then what's the definition of branding? Briefly, it's a company's effort to build lasting value by delighting customers. While the formulas for measuring brand value are complex, the goal of branding is simple: To delight customers so that MORE people buy MORE things for MORE years at a HIGHER price. Branding also has a karmic side. For example, if a company promises more than it delivers, its brand will suffer, which will cause the opposite effect: FEWER people buying FEWER things for FEWER years at a LOWER price. Companies serve at the pleasure of their customers.

ROSSER REEVES GOT ONE OUT OF THREE.

For many years Rosser Reeves worked at the Ted Bates agency, and in 1961 he wrote a book called REALITY IN ADVERTISING. In it he urged advertisers to focus all their communications on a Unique Selling Proposition, or USP, asserting that "the customer tends to remember just one thing from an advertisement—one strong claim, or one strong concept." While USP was a powerful idea in 1961, the only part of his phrase that seems powerful today is the "unique" part.

Customers today don't like to be sold—they like to buy, and they tend to buy in tribes. Better advice for companies is to focus their communications not on a USP but on a UBT—a Unique Buying Tribe—that has a natural affinity for the company's products or services. In a tribe, news spreads quickly, which gives brands extra traction.

USP was about PUSHING products and services. UBT is about PULLING people into a tribe they can trust. In a marketplace of me-too offerings, people don't seek features and benefits so much as tribal identity. "If I buy this product," they seem to ask, "what will that make me?"

THE TROUBLE WITH ADVERTISING.

Traditional advertising is in a death spiral. Media have splintered into smaller and smaller channels, so that it now costs too much to reach a large enough audience. But the root causes for the death spiral are twofold: 1) People don't like one-way conversations, and 2) People don't trust advertising. As a result, many are voting with their feet.

Traditional communication vehicles such as television commercials work best with intrusive, one-way selling messages. But since people now have a choice, they're choosing to spend more time on the Web, where communication is more like a conversation than a sales pitch. They're also listening more to their friends, in a return to the word-of-mouth culture that existed before mass communications. Unfortunately, as audiences turn their backs on intrusiveness, the advertising industry is fighting back with even more intrusiveness. This is the first reason for advertising's death spiral.

Traditional advertising also works best when the promise is large—larger than the product or

BY BEING MORE INTRUSIVE AND "HITTING BELOW THE BELT," TRADITIONAL ADVERTISING ACHIEVES SHORT-TERM GAINS AT THE RISK OF LONG-TERM EFFECTIVENESS.

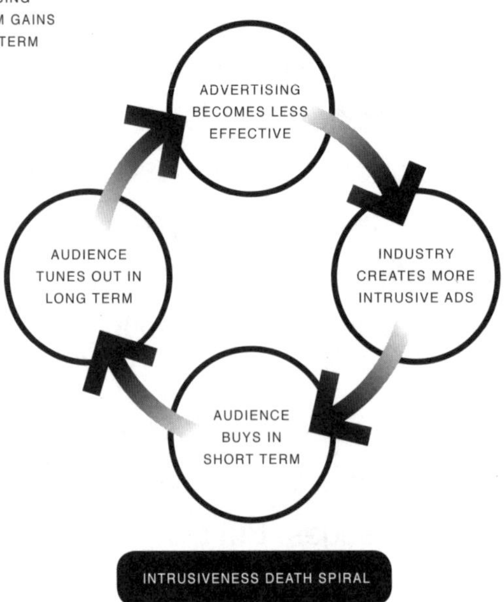
ADVERTISING BECOMES LESS EFFECTIVE
INDUSTRY CREATES MORE INTRUSIVE ADS
AUDIENCE BUYS IN SHORT TERM
AUDIENCE TUNES OUT IN LONG TERM

INTRUSIVENESS DEATH SPIRAL

service can deliver—which is why people long ago learned to distrust it. In a 1998 Gallup poll rating honesty and ethical standards across a range of professions, advertising people ended up near the bottom, sandwiched between lawyers and car salesmen. Today 92% of people skip the commercials on their recorded programs. How has the industry responded? By hitting further below the belt—sneaking advertising into editorial copy, television content, movies, and events, all under the euphemistic heading of product placement.

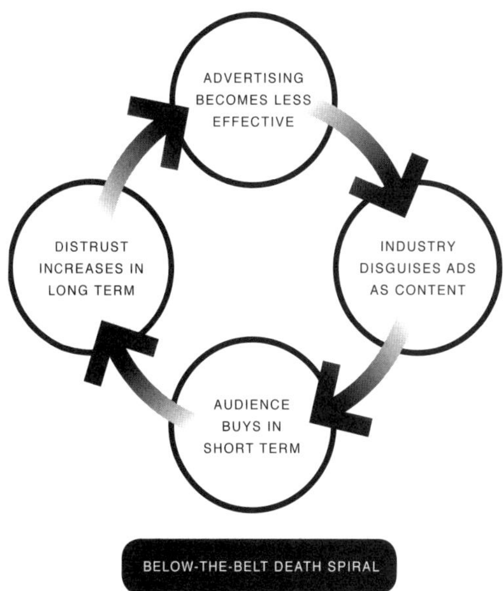
ADVERTISING BECOMES LESS EFFECTIVE
INDUSTRY DISGUISES ADS AS CONTENT
AUDIENCE BUYS IN SHORT TERM
DISTRUST INCREASES IN LONG TERM

BELOW-THE-BELT DEATH SPIRAL

This blurring of "church and state"—content and advertising—combined with exaggerated promises has created the second reason for advertising's death spiral.

Will the industry pull out of its tailspin? Probably, because advertising people are smart, and will find ways to reinvent their industry. Will it still be called advertising? That's another question. What people want today are trustworthy brands. What they don't want is more intrusiveness, more empty claims, more clutter.

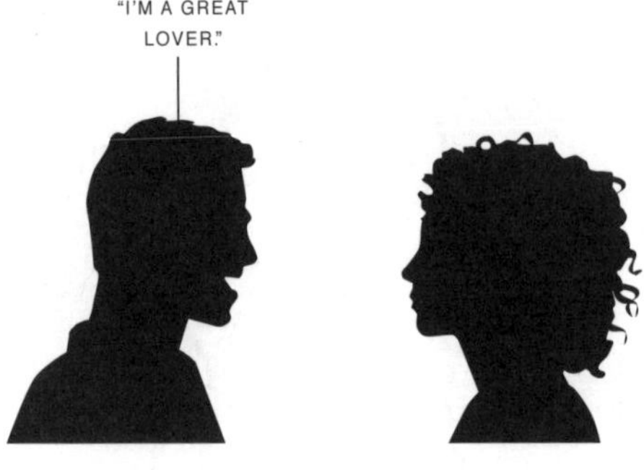

1. MARKETING

2. TELEMARKETING

3. PUBLIC RELATIONS

"I'M A GREAT LOVER.
I'M A GREAT LOVER.
I'M A GREAT LOVER."

4. ADVERTISING

5. GRAPHIC DESIGN

"I UNDERSTAND
YOU'RE A GREAT
LOVER."

6. BRANDING

DON'T OFFER MORE—OFFER DIFFERENT.

One day in 2005, the top two stories in THE WALL STREET JOURNAL were: 1) "The U.S. economy appears to have lost steam," and 2) "Apple's profit surges more than sixfold." The message was crystal clear to any CEO who happened to glance at the headlines that day: To succeed in a competitive business climate, you have to innovate. Apple's philosophy of "Think different" may turn out to be the mantra for 21st century business.

Differentiation, the art of standing out from the competition, is not front-page news. What IS front-page news, in a world of extreme clutter, is that you need more than differentiation. You need RADICAL differentiation.

The new rule: When everybody zigs, zag. Traditional differentiation is an uphill battle in which companies lavish too much effort on too few competitive advantages: the latest feature, a new color, a lower price, a higher speed. Radical differentiation, on the other hand, is about finding a whole new market space you can own and defend, thereby delivering profits over years instead of months.

Think of radical differentiation as the engine for a high-performance brand. It gets you on the fast track to having more people buy more stuff for more years at a higher price. It creates a strategic filter for questions such as "What should we do?" "What should we make?" "Who should we make it for?" "Who should we hire?" and "How should we behave?" With a zag, you can start a new category that your customers, your employees, your partners—even your competitors—will help you build. Without a zag, you could easily end up in the fossil layers of market clutter.

To deploy radical differentiation, you'll need to master four disciplines:

1. Finding your zag
2. Designing your zag
3. Renewing your zag

Ready?

BE DIFFERENT.

NO, **REALLY**

DIFFERENT.

PART 1 : FINDING YOUR ZAG

HIT 'EM WHERE THEY AIN'T.

When I was five, my dad bought me a kid-sized baseball bat and set out to teach me the great American game. As he pitched ball after ball, he served up a steady stream of advice. "Bend your knees. Elbows up. Watch the ball. Step into it. Level swing. Follow through." But the advice that comes back to me now is the advice he gave me later, when I asked him how I could improve my batting average. He said, "Hit 'em where they ain't."

Dad was echoing the words of Wee Willie Keeler, the smallest man in the history of baseball. At only 5'4" and 140 pounds, Keeler amassed a streak of 200-hit seasons that lasted from 1894 to 1902, and after 19 years in the major leagues he retired with a lifetime batting average of .347. What's more, he did it with a bat not much bigger than the one my father bought me when I was five. How? He used brains instead of brawn. He learned how to find the spaces between the fielders.

THE DYNAMICS OF DIFFERENT AND GOOD.

For most companies, the problem with radical differentiation is the "radical" part. If nobody's doing it, you'd be crazy to do it yourself, right? Wrong. In fact, if you're looking to become the leader in a new market space, the rule is just the opposite. If ANYBODY'S doing it, you'd be crazy to do it yourself. You can't be a leader by following the leader. Instead, you have to find the spaces between the fielders. You have to find a zag.

What stops most companies from zagging is the cloud of uncertainty that follows innovation. In an effort to remove the cloud, marketers often conduct focus groups, which, while helpful in some situations, are notably unhelpful for encouraging innovation. This is because radical differentiation doesn't test well in focus groups. When you ask people what they want, they'll invariably say they want more of the same, only with better features, a lower price, or both. This is not a recipe for radical differentiation. This is a recipe for me-too products with pint-sized profit potential.

A better way to judge a new offering is to map customer feedback against a success pattern. When you draw a chart with two axes, one for "good" and one for "different," you can see how your business concept stacks up against other successful zags. You can also begin to see why most companies are fooled by focus groups.

On the chart, the "good" axis can include any attributes that customers typically value: quality workmanship, good aesthetics, low price, high functionality, ease of use, speed, power, style, and so on. These are the qualities on which most offerings compete. The "different" axis is for any attributes that make an offering, well—different. These can include attributes that customers may characterize as surprising, weird, ugly, fresh, crazy, offbeat, novel, and so on.

As with other charts of this type, the best place to be is in the upper-right corner—in this case, where good and different combine to create a successful zag. Classic examples are the Aeron chair, Citibank, Toyota Prius, Charles Schwab, and Cirque du Soleil. However, successful zags usually test poorly with consumers before they're launched. They fare pretty well on the "good" axis, but then attract so many

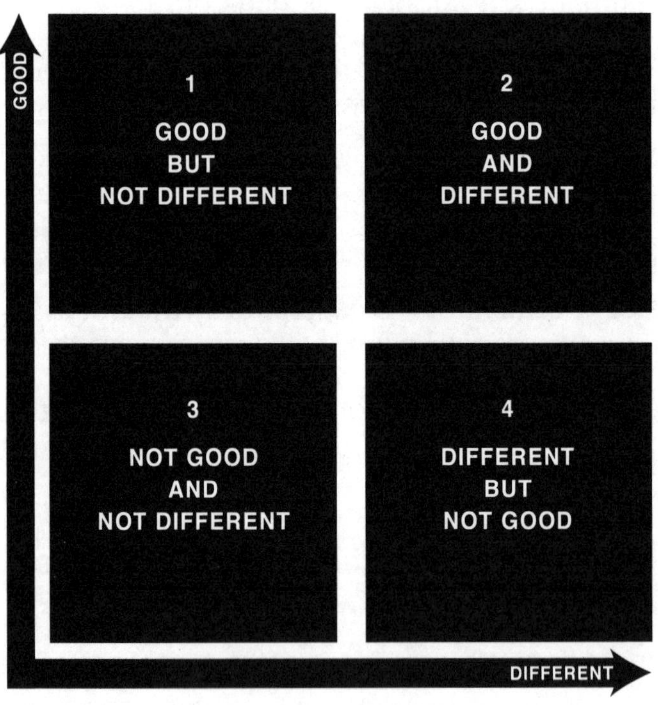
GOOD
1
GOOD
BUT
NOT DIFFERENT
2
GOOD
AND
DIFFERENT
3
NOT GOOD
AND
NOT DIFFERENT
4
DIFFERENT
BUT
NOT GOOD
DIFFERENT

GOOD

1 **GOOD BUT NOT DIFFERENT**	2 **GOOD AND DIFFERENT**
• DOES VERY WELL IN TESTS • GOES TO MARKET EASILY • GENERATES INCREMENTAL PROFITS UNTIL CHALLENGED BY COMPETITORS • EARNS SMALL MARKET SHARE • SOME BRAND POTENTIAL	• DOES POORLY IN TESTS • GOES TO MARKET W/ DIFFICULTY • CUSTOMERS SOON EQUATE "DIFFERENT" WITH "GOOD" • GENERATES LASTING PROFITS • EARNS LARGE MARKET SHARE • STRONG BRAND POTENTIAL
3 **NOT GOOD AND NOT DIFFERENT**	4 **DIFFERENT BUT NOT GOOD**
• DOES WELL IN TESTS • GOES TO MARKET EASILY • GENERATES INCREMENTAL PROFITS BUT EVENTUALLY FAILS IN MARKETPLACE • EARNS SMALL MARKET SHARE • LITTLE BRAND POTENTIAL	• DOES POORLY IN TESTS • GOES TO MARKET W/ DIFFICULTY • EVENTUALLY FAILS IN MARKETPLACE AS CUSTOMERS EQUATE "DIFFERENT" WITH "BAD" • EARNS NO MARKET SHARE • NO BRAND POTENTIAL

DIFFERENT

THE GOOD-DIFFERENT CHART HELPS YOU MATCH YOUR CUSTOMERS' REACTIONS TO SUCCESS PATTERNS, RATHER THAN TAKING THEIR COMMENTS AT FACE VALUE.

negative comments on the "different" axis that their companies get nervous and reject them.

Not surprisingly, where companies find the most encouragement is in the upper-left corner. Offerings here test extremely well, and the "good" comments are rarely undermined by negative comments such as "weird," "ugly," "offbeat," or "crazy." But the reason customers don't make negative comments about offerings in this corner is that there's nothing new or different to dislike. So while offerings in the upper-left may test extremely well, there's little chance that they'll lead to radical differentiation.

Offerings in the lower left corner, where "not good" meets "not different," test fairly well with customers, since there's not much to dislike or misunderstand about them. While this can encourage companies to proceed, in the end these offerings fail because there's either too little demand or too much competition.

Offerings in the lower right corner usually don't get off the ground at all. They're perceived from the start to be dogs—and guess what?—they are.

What makes the good-different chart tricky, though, is that some of the potential winners in the upper right corner look a lot like the dogs in the bottom right corner. The line is often blurry, and the consequences for making a bad call can be extreme. It takes an experienced innovator to know the difference—someone who can match customer comments to a previous pattern of success.

When BMW decided to launch the Mini Cooper, piles of research showed that Americans had no interest in an ultrasmall car and only wanted more SUVs. Despite this "fact," the zagmeisters at BMW stepped on the gas instead of the brakes and motored straight into profitable new market space.

The intrepid folks at BMW had a lot in common with physicist Niels Bohr. Many years ago one of his colleagues was invited to deliver a controversial paper to a group of scientists, including Bohr. Immediately afterward his colleague asked Bohr how the paper was received by the other scientists. He replied, "We all agree that your idea is crazy. What divides us is whether it is crazy enough." The Mini people were crazy, too. Like a fox.

LOOK FOR THE WHITE SPACE.

Finding open market space is a counterintuitive skill. The human perceptual system is only programmed to notice what's there, not what's not there. In perceptual theory, the difference between THERE and NOT THERE is known as figure and ground, or positive and negative space. Artists are trained to appreciate both at once, which may explain why they sometimes notice things that others don't. Companies need to think like artists when they're looking for new market space, because new market space, or "white space," is the secret to zagging.

Successful market spaces that were once white space include sticky notes (Post-Its), environmental music (Muzak), DVDs by mail (Netflix), military-style cars (Hummer), pre-fab designer houses (Dwell magazine), direct-to-customer computers (Dell), and point-to-point airlines (Southwest).

But what other offerings are "missing" from the brandscape? How about gourmet drive-through restaurants? Dinner-club movie theatres? Hourly nap rooms in airports? Wood-scented barbecue gas? A national pet-sitting service? Easy-to-change halogen bulbs? Whiteboard branding books? Wait—that one's already taken.

UNCOVER A NEED STATE.

A powerful technique for finding white space is to do what Clayton Christensen and Michael Raynor suggest in their book THE INNOVATOR'S SOLUTION: Look for a job people are already trying to get done, then help them do it. Jobs-based innovation, as opposed to product-based innovation, helps you get around the difficulty of testing a product that has yet to be commercialized.

A successful example of jobs-based innovation is the ten-dollar reading glasses you find in drugstores. The cheap-reader category was pure white space before someone noticed a job not getting done: People were going without extra pairs of glasses because they didn't want to spend hundreds of dollars on prescription pairs. Are the cheap readers as good as prescription glasses? No—but it doesn't matter. At 5% of the price of prescription glasses, the cheap readers do a good enough job. So good, in fact, that people buy pairs for every room in the house, and the category has become a half-billion-dollar industry.

A.G. Lafley, CEO of Procter & Gamble, has energized his company by putting a microscope on the need states of its consumers. Using

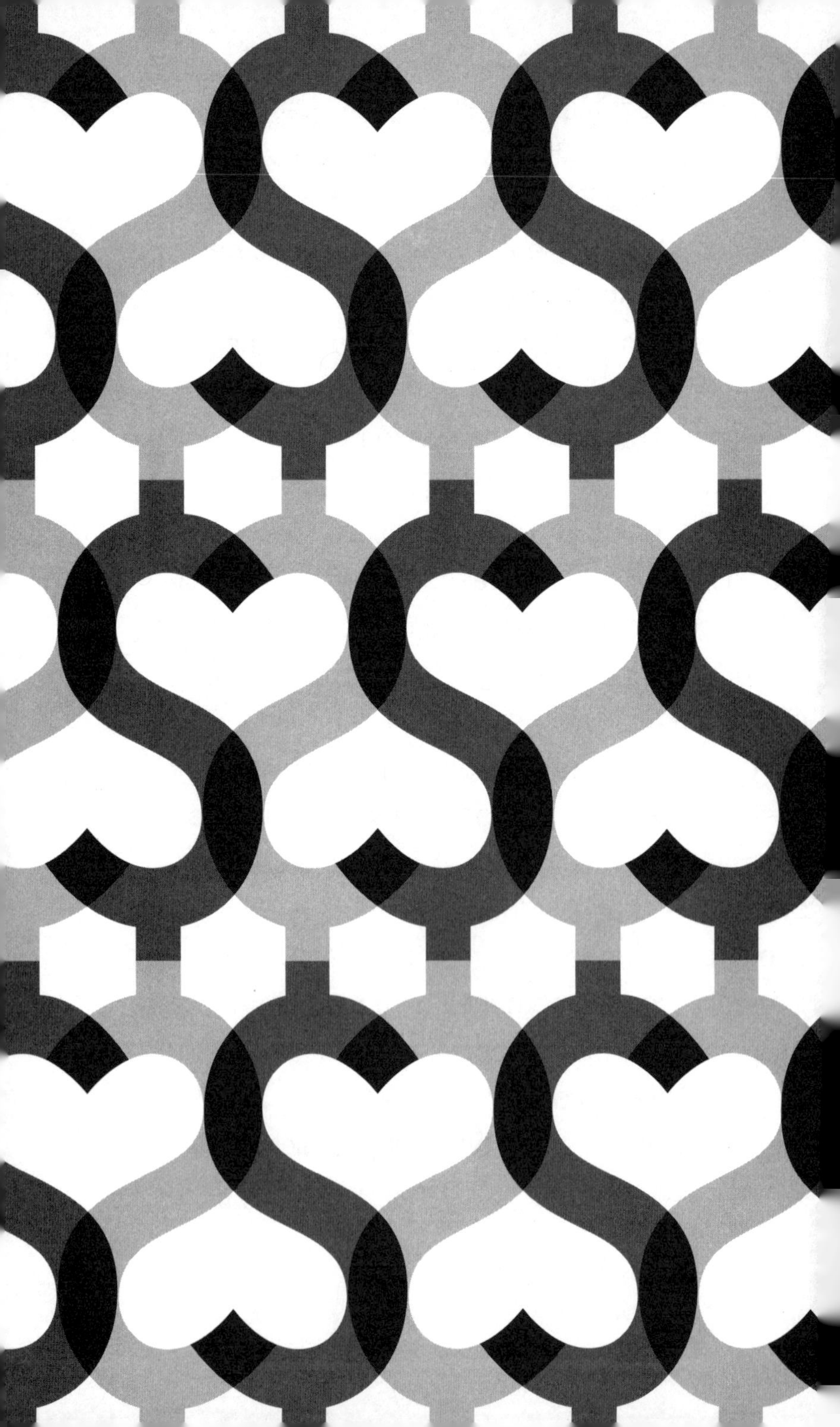

WHICH DID YOU SEE FIRST,
THE DOLLAR SIGNS OR
THE HEARTS?

ethnographic research in which researchers move in with consumers to observe their habits firsthand, they uncover need states like the one that led to their hugely successful Swiffer product. They noticed that the consumer had no easy way to spot-sweep dry spills without the hassle of a broom and dustpan—and found a solution that helped her get it done. "The simple principle in life," said Lafley, "is to find out what she wants and give it to her. It's worked in my marriage for 35 years and it works in laundry." When you're searching for a need state, don't think so much about the unbuilt product as about the unserved tribe.

Of course, brands get an extra boost when they're powered by trends. Starbucks got a boost from the trend toward a more European lifestyle. The Apple iPod got a boost from the trend toward online music sharing. Charles Schwab got a boost from the trend toward more customized personal investing. Whole Foods and Trader Joe's got a boost from the trend toward organic living. Tout Beau, Jean-Paul Gaultier's line of male cosmetics, got a boost from the trend toward metrosexuality. And Axe Body Spray got a boost from an equal and opposite trend toward macho-sexuality.

FIND A PARADE.

I have a vivid memory of standing in the kitchen one afternoon, home from high-school baseball practice, jars rattling faintly in the open fridge. I never showed the potential of a Willie Keeler, so I was drowning my sorrows in a quart of milk.

"Tell me," said my mother. "How do you see your future?"

I said, "I don't know. I feel like I could be a leader of something—I'm just not sure what."

She thought. "Well, that's not so hard. Just find a parade and get in front of it."

These two pieces of advice, one each from my father and mother would make a nice set of bookends for a brand library. Between hitting 'em where they ain't (differentiation) and getting in front of a parade (finding a trend), you have the keys to finding your zag. Now all you need is a process for building it into a high-performance brand.

PART 2 : DESIGNING YOUR ZAG

BRAND AS A SYSTEM.

In my earlier book, THE BRAND GAP, I showed that brand-building isn't a series of isolated activities, but a complete system in which five disciplines—differentiation, collaboration, innovation, validation, and cultivation—combine to produce a sustainable competitive advantage. My intent with ZAG is to zoom in on differentiation to reveal the system within the system.

While the previous section gave you clues for finding your zag, this section offers a process for designing it. I use the word design as economist Herbert Simon used it: "Everyone designs who devises courses of action aimed at changing existing situations into preferred ones." The preferred situation in this case is a compelling brand based on radical differentiation. The course of action is a brand strategy that zags.

All design relies on heuristic thinking more than algorithmic thinking—meaning that there is no set path, no mathematical formula, for reaching your goal. But you still need rigor and process, otherwise you'll drift from one thought to the next with no more hope of it making sense than the proverbial thousand monkeys with their thousand typewriters.

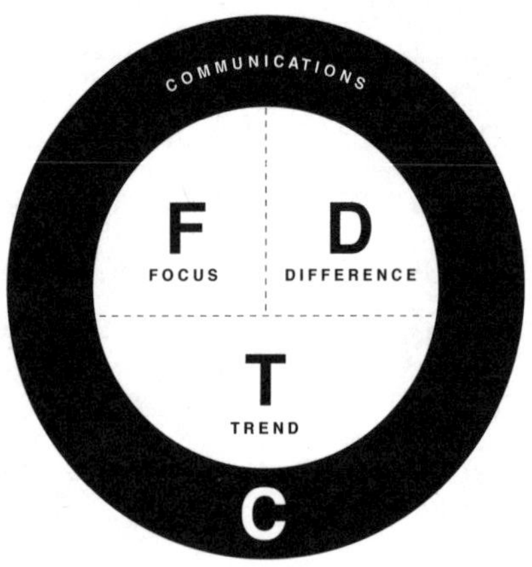

WHEN FOCUS IS PAIRED WITH DIFFERENTIATION, SUPPORTED BY A TREND, AND SURROUNDED BY COMPELLING COMMUNICATIONS, YOU HAVE THE BASIC INGREDIENTS OF A ZAG.

In this section I'll share the 17 checkpoints we use at Neutron to coach our clients through the zag design process. Each checkpoint addresses one of four key elements—differentiation, focus, trend, and communications—indicated by the small diagram at the end of each checkpoint.

To demonstrate how the 17-step process works, I've included examples from an exercise we use in our branding workshops. The object is to build a brand for a fictitious chain of wine bars. Of course, no single example can stand in for the entire range of brand types, but it should help you to visualize the leap from principles to practice.

Checkpoint 1: WHO ARE YOU?

The first step in building a brand is to look inside and see where the raw energy will come from. White space has little value without the experience, credibility, and passion needed to fuel success day after day, year after year, under the pressure of competition. Joseph Campbell's advice to "follow your bliss" applies as much to companies as it does to individuals.

To prove this principle, let's look at what happens when passion is removed from the equation. Remember the dot-com disasters of the nineties? There was plenty of passion for stock options, but little passion for building a real company to serve the long-term good of a community. As a result, we saw the proliferation of "junk brands"—brands with beguiling fronts but nothing real to back them up. The economy soon collapsed, taking the junk brands with it. The words of investor-philosopher Warren Buffett suddenly rang true. "When the tide goes out, you can see who's wearing bathing suits."

For contrast, let's look at a dot-com business that has passion behind it—Google. While Google has certainly made people rich, the founders have built the brand on a clearly stated moral code: "Don't be evil." This clear philosophy has allowed the company not only to survive the dot-com bust, but to inspire employees, delight users, and attract investors—to a degree no one thought possible.

And what about your company? Where's your passion? One way to bring it into sharp relief is by completing the exercise that the corporate story experts at C2 (San Francisco) give to their clients to help them shape their visions. It goes like this: 25 years from now your company is wiped out. Now, sit down and write your company's obituary. What would you like posterity to say about you? You'll find that the answers are also the answers to the seminal questions: Who are you? Where does your passion lie? What gets you up in the morning?

Now let's go to our wine bar. We start the journey with a small group of partners who have a common passion: They love wine, food, travel—and long to share that love with the rest of the world. Their passion is strong enough to get them over a number of hurdles, both seen and unseen, and they have enough experience and credibility to be taken seriously by customers, partners, and investors. They have just cleared checkpoint 1.

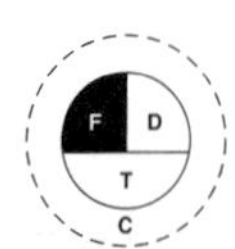

OBITUARY

World Mourns Tastings

Tastings (name to come), the chain of wine bars that introduced millions of people to the culture of wine, closed its doors last Friday. It ran an enormously successful and popular business for 25 years.

From a single wine bar in Napa Valley, the company grew rapidly to over 400 locations across America, from San Diego to Boston, Seattle to Miami. It soon extended the brand to the Australasia market, and later South America, South Africa, and eastern Europe. Tastings Inc. closed with cash and assets worth in excess of 1.2 billion dollars, a sum the company says it will donate to causes that include third-world education, sustainable farming, and international peace.

The founders had launched Tastings with a simple hope—that learning about wine would bring the world closer together. Their goal was to foster an "international cafe society" by promoting conversation, community, and cultural understanding among people. By delivering education along with tastes of wine, they created an atmosphere that encouraged the sharing of experiences among customers.

Some business observers have asked why Tastings is closing its doors before entering lucrative markets such as western Europe. Explained one of the founders, "We achieved o goal ahead of schedule. The world is well it's way toward warmer relations, and doe need us anymore."

May they rest in peace.

MICROSOFT
TO PUT A COMPUTER ON EVERY DESK AND IN EVERY HOME

CIRQUE DU SOLEIL
TO INVOKE THE IMAGINATION, PROVOKE THE SENSES, AND EVOKE THE EMOTIONS OF PEOPLE AROUND THE WORLD

AUTODESK
TO CREATE SOFTWARE TOOLS THAT TRANSFORM IDEAS INTO REALITY

KELLOGG'S
TO MAKE QUALITY PRODUCTS FOR A HEALTHIER WORLD

KAUFMAN AND BROAD
TO BUILD HOMES THAT MEET PEOPLE'S DREAMS

COCA-COLA
TO REFRESH THE WORLD

Checkpoint 2: WHAT DO YOU DO?

Next you need to clarify what business you're in—your core purpose. Core purpose, according to BUILT TO LAST authors Jim Collins and Jerry Porras, is the fundamental reason your company exists beyond making money. It's the one thing that will never change about your business. For example, Google's stated purpose is to organize the world's information and make it universally accessible; Disney's purpose is to make people happy. These are very different companies, but what they have in common is a clear sense of who they are and why they're doing what they do. Without a clear sense of purpose, companies tend to grab at short-term gains while incurring the long-term loss of their identities.

The partners in the wine bar have gotten their purpose statement down to seven words: To bring people together through wine education. While someday they could make small adjustments to their purpose, they've agreed on a differentiating idea—education.

How many words will it take to articulate your purpose? If it takes more than 12, go back to checkpoint 1, or set it aside and return to it later.

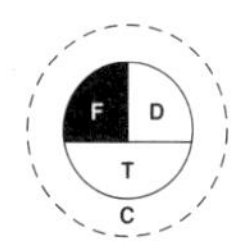

Checkpoint 3: WHAT'S YOUR VISION?

A company's core purpose gives it a heading, a direction toward the future. While a company's purpose can be abstract, a company's vision should be concrete. It's an illustration of the future—a picture shared by the entire company. "A soul never thinks without an image," said Aristotle, and a company never acts without a vision.

The word "vision" is tossed around a lot in business today, but often what passes for vision is merely the LEADER'S vision. True vision can't be imposed on a company—it has to grow from the shared purpose and passion of its people. The leader's job is to shape and articulate that vision, making it palpable, memorable, inspiring. True vision leads to commitment rather than compliance, confidence rather than caution.

The relationship between purpose and vision was explained vividly by Peter Senge in THE FIFTH DISCIPLINE. Referring to the Kennedy years, he said a purpose is "advancing man's capabilities to explore the heavens." A vision, on the other hand, is "a man on the moon by the end of the 1960s." Everyone could picture that man, up there on the moon, planting an American flag in the soft sand.

Without a clearly drawn vision, it's dangerous to empower people. It only leads to confusion, anxiety, and distrust as employees work at cross-purposes, often taking refuge in functional silos instead of collaborating to transform a shared picture of the future into reality.

How do you shape a vision? The "vision designers" at Stone Yamashita Partners advise their clients to produce vision deliverables: a brochure, a script, an important speech—anything that forces them to articulate their vision to the outside world. When you put your vision to paper, you can immediately see its flaws. Then you can reinforce it to withstand the slings and arrows that test the resolve of any organization.

Back at the wine bar, the partners are busy sketching a picture of their own company's future. They envision at least one Tastings (name to come) in every college town across America. Each bar has a hundred wines from around the world, all available by the glass, in a constantly changing menu of varietals and producers. They see happy groups of people learning about wine, talking about wine, and swapping stories about food, travel, and the cultures they've experienced.

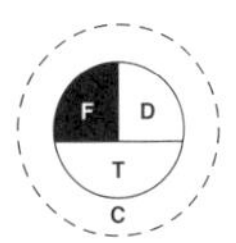

Checkpoint 4: WHAT WAVE ARE YOU RIDING?

The first three checkpoints illustrate the role of focus in building a zag. The next five checkpoints will show how focus connects to its powerful twin, differentiation. But let's take a break for a moment to consider the role of trends in driving both.

You can certainly build a brand without harnessing a trend, but you won't get the raw, youthful energy of a zag. When focus and differentiation are powered by a trend, the result is a charismatic brand that customers wouldn't trade for love nor money. It's the difference between paddling a surfboard and riding a wave.

What trends can you ride? The variety is virtually endless, since each industry, region, and subculture spawns its own trends. Sometimes a trend is a reaction to a previous trend that has lost its cachet, such as the way rock stars replaced crooners in the fifties. Other times it's the result of a technological innovation, such as the manufactured molecule Kevlar igniting a revolution in textile manufacturing. Some trends, such as democracy, are still gaining strength after hundreds of years, while others, such as body piercing, may end up as a half page in the history of fashion.

Examples of current trend-riders are Samsung with high-design gadgets, Anthropologie with eclectic clothing, Progressive with self-service insurance, Dean & Deluca with gourmet groceries, Aveda with prestige eco-friendly cosmetics, Design Within Reach with neo-Modernist furniture, and Volkswagen with its new "transparent" factory and car-recycling facility. When you look under the hood of a high-performance brand, you almost always find it's powered by a trend.

Trend power is increased when a brand rides more than one trend at a time. Our fictitious wine bar is riding several—the trends toward the democratization of wine, international travel, sustainable farming, affordable luxury, and gourmet food. With a little work, it could also ride the trends toward integrated technology, experience design, self-service, and duty-free shopping. It could also ride wine industry microtrends such as the trend toward low-priced wines, location-specific wines, or corkless packaging.

Trends are the tides that lift all boats.

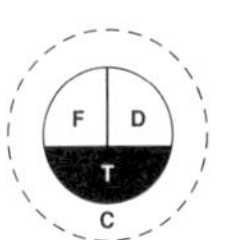

AUTHENTICITY
ORGANIC FOOD
MINIATURIZATION
LONGEVITY
BODY ENHANCEMENT
GREEN LIVING
HEALTH CARE
PERSONAL TECHNOLOGY
OPENNESS
DEMOCRACY
AFFORDABLE LUXURY
HIGH DESIGN
HOME CREATIVITY
OUTSOURCING
MOBILE COMPUTING
SELF-SERVICE
PERSONAL CREATIVITY
ONLINE SHOPPING

SIMPLICITY
GOURMET COOKING
SUSTAINABILITY
ENVIRONMENTAL RESPONSIBILITY
DESIGN
NOSTALGIA
WORLD TRAVEL
INSTANT COMMUNICATION
SPIRITUALITY
SLOW FOOD MOVEMENT
METROSEXUALITY
ON-DEMAND TECHNOLOGY
PROFESSIONAL-GRADE TOOLS
NEO-MODERNISM
MENTAL FITNESS
PET SERVICES
EASTERN INFLUENCES
INTERACTIVE ENTERTAINMENT

Checkpoint 5: WHO SHARES THE BRANDSCAPE?

A brand doesn't exist in a vacuum. The passion, purpose, and vision that drive a company may be virtually identical with those of competitors. You've probably seen the lists of core values that companies publish to help them define their cultures. When you look at these lists across an industry, they appear to be selected from a short list of about 12 virtues. Our company's culture is (choose four): innovative, market-driven, customer-focused, ethical, responsive, collaborative, trusted, quality-minded, progressive, proactive, responsible, and optimistic.

While virtues like these are admirable, zagging requires that a company define itself by what makes it UNIQUE, not what makes it admirable. Here we need to leave the realm of focus and enter the territory of differentiation.

Every competitive category has its winners and losers. In brand building, winning and losing is relative, since there may be room for three, four, or even more brands to exist profitably in one category. But what's especially interesting about competitive categories is how they tend to arrange themselves into predictable hierarchies.

In a mature category, what you often find is that the number-one brand has roughly twice the market share of the number-two brand, which has roughly twice the share of the number-three brand, which has roughly twice the share of the number-four brand, and so on, until there's no market left to share. In categories that support more competitors, the differential between the market shares is less dramatic, but the hierarchy is still intact.

This phenomenon conforms to what network theorists call "power laws"—laws that explain why success attracts success, or why "the rich get richer." In the world of power laws, market-share hierarchies are controlled by customers, who collectively determine the success order of competitors. Success order, in turn, is determined by two factors: the "birth order" of competitors, which includes the much-touted "first-mover advantage," and "preferential attachment," the network theorists' term for popularity. As positioning experts Jack Trout and Al Ries have often stated, the biggest winner is not the brand that's first into the marketplace, but the one that's first into people's minds.

Given the presence of power laws, the only positions worth owning in most categories are numbers one and two. Number three might be a useful position from which to unseat number two. Below number three, however, it usually makes more sense to start a new category than to battle the top three incumbents. The list on page 64 describes some of the circumstances that activate power laws in favor of the leading brand. Jack Welch clearly understood the power of market leadership in 1981 when he told his business heads to "fix, sell, or close" any GE division that wasn't either one or two in its category.

The power law that governs brand leadership can be reduced to a simple formula:

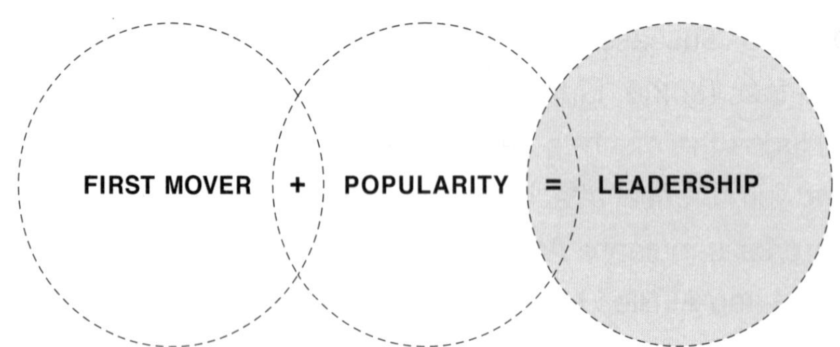

Some brands are especially susceptible to power laws, such as those that act as "hubs" in a technological, industrial, or social network. The reason Microsoft is so strongly positioned in the marketplace is that the marketplace doesn't really want another standard for operating systems. It's the same reason that Microsoft will find it difficult to unseat Adobe in document portability. One PDF standard is enough.

But what about the wine bar? What category will it attempt to lead? Since a chain of educational wine bars is a new concept, it has a chance to be the first-mover in a new category, with leadership guaranteed in the short term. In the long term, however, it will need to achieve the second part of the power law—popularity—to remain the leader when competitors enter the category.

Of course, the wine bar will have a certain amount of competition even before it establishes a new category. In the beginning it will compete with existing alternatives such as traditional bars, self-service wine bars, tasting rooms, wineshops, and restaurants. Therefore it's crucial that it be born with a fully formed zag.

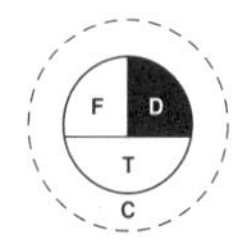

CIRCUMSTANCES THAT FAVOR THE LEADING BRAND:

1 when the CATEGORY is confusing (cell phones)

2 when COMPARISON is difficult (advertising agencies)

3 when the PRICE is high (automobiles)

4 when the INTEREST level is low (table salt)

5 when a STANDARD is needed (operating systems)

6 when the BENEFITS are intangible (banking)

7 when the FEATURES are technical (pharmaceuticals)

8 when the ADVANTAGES are unprovable (jewelry)

9 when the RISK factor is high (law firms)

10 when customers want PRESTIGE (fashion)

Checkpoint 6: WHAT MAKES YOU THE "ONLY"?

Complete this sentence: Our brand is the ONLY __________ that __________. In the first blank, put the name of your category (frozen pizza, furniture dealership, computer repair service). In the second blank, describe your zag (that tastes like Naples; that sells sustainably manufactured furniture; that makes house calls). If you can't keep it brief and use the word ONLY, then you don't have a zag. Your best option in that case is to make a list of all the competitors who could make the same claim, then start to shift your strategy away from theirs.

Remember, a zag is not merely differentiation, but RADICAL differentiation. So when my local bank bought a fifty-foot outdoor poster emblazoned with the tagline, "Nice. Since 1878," they'd have been better off putting their money in a savings account. "Nice" is not a zag, and neither is "1878." A zag is what Citibank did when they positioned their company as the anti-bank with the tagline, "Live richly," and headlines such as, "For a guaranteed return on investment, try buying flowers."

"Onliness" is the true test of a zag. If you can't say you're the "only," go back and start over.

Does the wine bar concept pass the onliness test? Let's try it. "Our brand is the ONLY chain of wine bars that builds community around wine education." Yep. That works. Even with this simple statement you can see that there are three unique attributes that will set the brand apart: It's a chain instead of a one-off; it's about community, not just customers; and it's built on education, not just enjoyment.

Now that you've got the principle, here's a more detailed version of the exercise to help you pinpoint your onliness. It parallels the journalistic model of storytelling: WHAT is your category? HOW are you different? WHO are your customers? WHERE are they located? WHEN do they need you? and WHY are you important?

FOR HARLEY-DAVIDSON

WHAT:	The ONLY motorcycle manufacturer
HOW:	that makes big, loud motorcycles
WHO:	for macho guys (and macho "wannabees")
WHERE:	mostly in the United States
WHY:	who want to join a gang of cowboys
WHEN:	in an era of decreasing personal freedom

FOR WHEAT MONTANA FARMS

WHAT: The ONLY wheat distributor
HOW: that sells grind-it-yourself wheat in stores
WHO: for serious home bakers
WHERE: in the United States
WHY: who want fresh-ground flour for baking
WHEN: in an era of growing interest in “slow food”

FOR THE WHITE STRIPES

WHAT: The ONLY pop music duo
HOW: that records crude yet hip rock songs
WHO: for young urbanites
WHERE: in the U.S. and other first-world countries
WHY: who long for authenticity
WHEN: in an era of overproduced, me-too music

FOR HOOTERS

WHAT: The ONLY chain of restaurants
HOW: that hires overtly sexy waitresses
WHO: for young male customers
WHERE: in the United States
WHY: who want to indulge their libidos
WHEN: in an era of strict political correctness

Notice the extra detail yielded by this format. You not only get the category (WHAT) and the point of differentiation (HOW), but you also segment the audience (WHO), narrow your market geography (WHERE), focus on a need state (WHY), and define the underlying trend (WHEN). Now let's go back to the wine bar.

FOR THE WINE BAR

WHAT:	The ONLY chain of wine bars
HOW:	that builds community around education
WHO:	for men and women of drinking age
WHERE:	in cities and progressive towns in the U.S.
WHY:	who want to learn more about wine
WHEN:	in an era of cultural awakening

An onliness statement provides a framework for your zag. Once you've defined your point of differentiation, you have a decisional filter for all your company's future decisions. By checking back against your statement you can quickly see whether any new decision will help or hurt, focus or unfocus, purify or modify your brand.

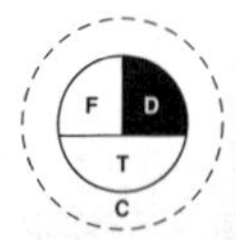

OUR ▬▬▬▬

IS THE **ONLY**

▬▬▬▬

THAT ▬▬▬▬.

GUSS
PICKLES

A SPECIALTY STORE IN A BIG CITY
AND A GENERAL STORE IN A SMALL TOWN
MUST ADHERE TO THE SAME PRINCIPLE:
THE WIDER THE COMPETITION,
THE NARROWER THE FOCUS—AND VICE VERSA.

Checkpoint 7: WHAT SHOULD YOU ADD OR SUBTRACT?

One of the most powerful principles in building a brand is focused alignment. Unfortunately, it's a principle honored more in the breach than in the observance. Why? Because we humans are more adept at adding elements than subtracting them. We LOVE to start new initiatives and build, build, build. We HATE being told "no." The principle of alignment, by contrast, is best served by extreme focus and self-discipline.

Brand alignment is the practice of linking your business strategy to customer experience—aligning all your company behaviors behind a clearly articulated zag. There should be no leftover parts, no maverick offerings, no contradiction between what you say and what you do. The result of alignment is coherence; the result of nonalignment is wasted resources.

In our workshops we demonstrate alignment using "the sacrifice game." In this exercise teams of participants start with a well-known brand, decide what makes it different and desirable, then prune back the brand to its core meaning by removing unaligned elements. Only then do the teams suggest new elements that might increase—not decrease—the focus of the brand. Thus they might decide that Ralph Lauren Polo stands for "classic upscale American clothing." To increase brand alignment, they might suggest that the company keep the clothing and accessories, but drop elements such as dog gifts, wall paint, furniture, TV show, magazines, and restaurants. They might then suggest adding one or two elements such as luggage or equestrian clothing.

The rule of thumb is simple: If adding an element to your brand brings you into competition with a stronger competitor, think twice. You may well end up wasting energy and confusing your customers in the bargain.

Consider the case of GM, who recently licensed its Cadillac logo to Kent International to create Cadillac Bicycles. According to the Cadillac folks, "This is the perfect way to break through preconceptions of what [customers] think they know about Cadillac." Exactly. Now they'll think that Cadillac is a luxury car and bicycle company. Why not just stay focused and build a better American luxury car? There's still plenty of room at the top. Lou Gerstner, former CEO of IBM, was fond of saying, "If you don't know where you're going, any

WHICH ONE IS THE CADILLAC?

direction will get you there." Cadillac saw the fork in the road, and took it.

How should our wine bar be aligned? Of course, since we're still in the conceptual stage, there are no mistakes to correct or elements to sacrifice. But there is an opportunity to "pre-sacrifice" a few assumptions. One assumption is that wine should cost about $7 a glass. Who says? If the brand is based on wine education, the "students" could end up spending more than they did on college. How about a range of "learning wines" for $2 a glass? Another assumption is that wine should always come in bottles. What if we put our "learning wines" in boxes that slow down oxidation? Or let customers bring in their own empty bottles as they do in some parts of Europe? We could then dispense "fresh wine" from stainless steel containers for a much lower price. Another assumption is that a wine bar should look like a winery, with lots of stone, rough wood, and leaded glass. Who says? What if it looked like a college library instead?

The quickest route to a zag is to look at what competitors do, then do something different.

No—REALLY different.

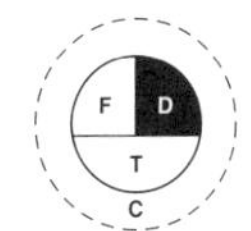

Checkpoint 8: WHO LOVES YOU?

Every brand is built by a community. Not just the community of people inside the company, but its partners, suppliers, investors, customers, non-customers, and even competitors. It's a complete ecosystem in which there are gives and gets all around. Everyone has a role to play, and everyone should be repaid for their efforts.

Let me illustrate this point with a story.

Most mornings I take my dog for a latté at a local café. The latté is for me—Boodles gets a biscuit. The café is nothing much, just a mom-and-pop retail shop in a strip mall, with bare concrete floors, a row of amateur photos on the wall, some scruffy couches on one side, a big coffee-roasting machine on the other side, and parking in front. The place is run by a nice Middle Eastern couple who keep it humming 365 days a year, except for a half-day off at Christmas.

On my first day there I was confronted with a long line. Yet, surprisingly, the line moved briskly. Not only that, everyone seemed to know everyone else's name. After a few more visits, I started to catch on. They had a "loyalty program"—a little paper card that gives you 12 drinks for the price of 10. They write your name and your favorite drink on the card, then punch it every time you order.

The result of this system is that everyone gets to know your name, and soon you know everyone else's name. Not only that, the counter people learn to recognize your car when you pull into the parking lot, so they have your drink ready when you get to the head of the line. Over time, little cliques of customers form and reform to chat with each other—over there on the couch, then at this table, that table, outside on the porch.

The advance team from Starbucks couldn't help but notice all the activity at the café, and they soon opened a beautifully appointed store on the same block. Do you remember where you were on September 11, 2001? I do. I was parking my car at the café, just weeks after the new Starbucks opened. Among the thoughts that flashed through my mind: These poor people—between the cultural backlash and the new Starbucks, they're history. So I resolved to lend my moral support by coming in the next day, rain or shine. When I pulled into the parking lot, my jaw dropped—the line of customers stretched out the door and around the building.

What is it that spawns such loyalty? How could this little place build the type of community that Starbucks only dreams of? Simple. It's in the gives and gets. The owners work hard so they can make a decent living. Customers come in every day so they can make new friends. The freelance baker makes special pastries so she can have a happy, fast-paying client. The landlord gives the café lower rent so it will attract customers for the other tenants. I get my latté and Boodles gets her biscuit. Meanwhile, Starbucks does only a modest business on the same block.

Could the wine bar profit from similar thinking? What will the customers get from joining the tribe? How about the employees? The wine producers? The neighboring shops at each location? The local cops (who may have to be called from time to time)? The local school system? Community charities? The investors, partners, and suppliers who help build the brand? The wine industry as a whole? To keep the system healthy and growing, everyone needs to contribute, and everyone needs to benefit.

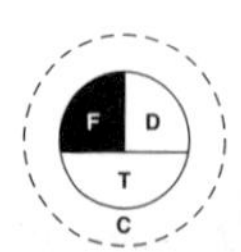

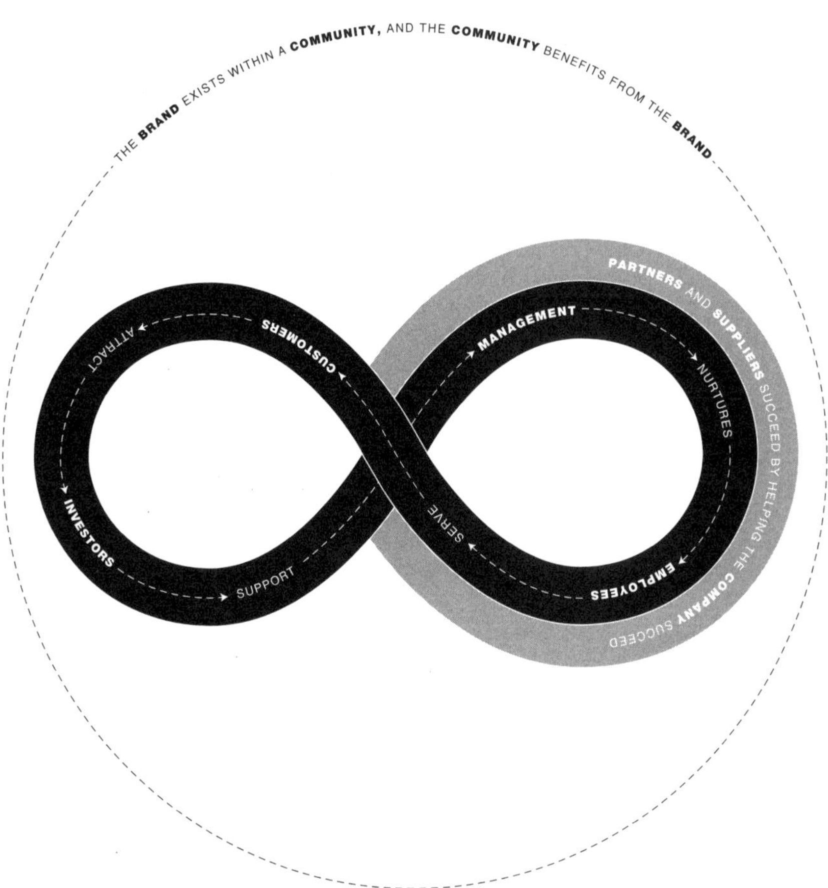
THE BRAND EXISTS WITHIN A COMMUNITY, AND THE COMMUNITY BENEFITS FROM THE BRAND
CUSTOMERS
ATTRACT
INVESTORS
SUPPORT
MANAGEMENT
NURTURES
EMPLOYEES
SERVE
PARTNERS AND SUPPLIERS SUCCEED BY HELPING THE COMPANY SUCCEED

A BRAND IS PART OF AN ECOSYSTEM IN WHICH EACH PARTICIPANT CONTRIBUTES AND EACH PARTICIPANT BENEFITS.

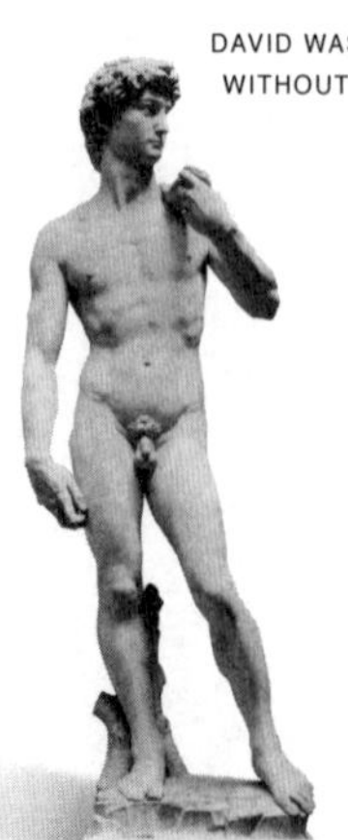

DAVID WAS NOTHING
WITHOUT GOLIATH.

Checkpoint 9: WHO'S THE ENEMY?

Everyone can't be your friend. Rather than trying to please everyone at the risk of pleasing no one, step right up and pick a fight. Just make sure you take on the biggest, most successful competitor you can find. Why? Because it puts the RADICAL in radical differentiation. Brand history abounds with evidence that David can take on Goliath and win—Avis taking on Hertz, Apple taking on IBM, the tiny Mini taking on the giant SUVs. The goal is not to topple the big guys, but to employ the principle of contrast to throw your zag into sharp relief.

Sometimes the enemy is not a competing company but the old way of doing things. Point it out! Point out to doctors that in handling their own bookkeeping they may be losing half their profits. Point out to travelers that $200 for a hotel room may be twice the value of a night's rest. Point out to supply chain managers that using faxes and sticky notes instead of software may be costing their company millions.

The enemy of the wine bar? How about the "priesthood" of wine snobs who use the mystique of wine to inflate prices and intimidate people? Let the revolution begin!

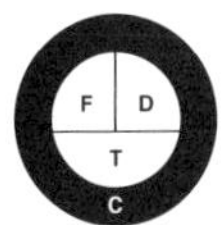

Checkpoint 10: WHAT DO THEY CALL YOU?

It's an ironic fact of marketing that a brand's most valuable asset is often the one given the least attention—its name. Maybe this is because new products, services, and companies are often christened before marketing teams are in place. Maybe it's because the founders believe it's their entrepreneurial privilege to name their own children. Or maybe it's because they aren't aware of the widening costs of a poorly named brand, or the streamlining effects of a well-named one.

Let's imagine a tale of two companies, both entering the highly competitive market for personal electronics. One is named Personal Media Devices, and the other is named Yubop.

The founders of Personal Media Devices are extremely pleased with their company name, because, as one executive put it, "It says it all. One look at the name and people will know exactly what we sell."

Now let's fast-forward five years. Personal Media Devices faces increasing competition from companies whose names are International Media Devices, Personal Media Systems, and International Media Machines. In addition, people have quickly tired of saying "Personal Media Devices" and now call the company "PMD." New customers have little idea of what PMD stands for, and are easily confused by its similarity to companies called PMC, DMD, and PDM, as well as their actual competitors, whose names people have already shortened to IMD, PMS, and IMM. Confused yet? PMD's customers are.

To differentiate themselves from the competition, PMD now spends an increasing amount of money on advertising and public relations to remind people that their company was one of the first and still the best. Even so, people can't remember if it's a PMD product that they wanted or a PMC product. PMD responds to increasing competition by decreasing its prices, and soon has to decrease its advertising budget as well. Meanwhile, a competitor called Yubop is causing the company fits.

The founders of Yubop were chided when they first proposed the name. As one investor said, "It just doesn't sound like a serious company." Yet, on the basis of its brevity, differentiation, and URL availability, they decided to go forward with it.

Five years later, Yubop is a household word. The tagline "Who bop?" has become one of the

STRONG AND WEAK NAMES

CATEGORIES	STRONG NAMES	WEAK NAMES
retail bank	Citibank	First Bank & Trust
movie studio	Dreamworks	United Artists
shipping	FedEx	DHL
SUV model	4Runner	Touareg
skin products	Olay	Noxzema
farm equipment	John Deere	AGCO
investing	Charles Schwab	Wachovia
magazine	Dwell	Architectural Digest
sports apparel	Under Armour	InSport
cat food	Meow Mix	Eukanuba
bus service	Greyhound	Intercity Transit
PDA	BlackBerry	Anextec SP230
coffee/tea shop	Starbucks	Coffee Bean & Tea Leaf
cellular service	Orange	MetroPCS
natural care	Burt's Bees	Herbal Luxuries
refrigerator	Sub-Zero	Thermador
law firm	Orrick	Wilson Sonsini Goodrich & Rosati
office equipment	Xerox	Kyocera Mita
online payments	PayPal	Click & Buy
network storage	Brocade	Network Storage Corporation
oil and gas	Shell	Unocal
erectile drug	Viagra	Cialis
billing service	Department B	American Billing Service
car model	Crossfire	Achieva
car insurance	Progressive	GEICO
internet voice	Lingo	iConnectHere
jams and jellies	Smuckers	Mary Ellen
TV search	MeeVee	Blinkx.TV
office supplies	Staples	OfficeMart
women's TV	We	Romance Classics
PC sound card	Mockingboard	Terratec EWS64 XL
optical lenses	Carl Zeiss	Sony Lenses
life insurance	MetLife	American United
Web search	Google	Ask

For my critique of these names, go to www.zagbook.com/namecrit.

most familiar phrases in advertising, with people using it in their everyday conversations. The Yubop creative community finds endless ways to play with the name in customer communications ("I bop, we bop, they bop, Yubop"), and word of mouth is now so strong that the company's marketing budget is considerably lower than the national average, while profit margins are higher.

Can a name do all that? Just ask Starbucks, jetBlue, TomTom (portable navigation), Brocade (storage networks), and Smuckers (jam). A poor name is a drag on the brand building process, but a good name accelerates it.

If your brand name is already locked in, you can move to the next checkpoint. If not, here are some quick tips for naming from THE BRAND GAP. A name should be: 1) different than those of competitors, 2) brief—four syllables or less, 3) appropriate, but not so descriptive that it sounds generic, 4) easy to spell, 5) satisfying to pronounce, 6) suitable for "brandplay," and 7) legally defensible.

Meanwhile, back at the wine bar, the founders have worked hard to improve on their temporary name, Tastings. Their final choice? Turn the page and see.

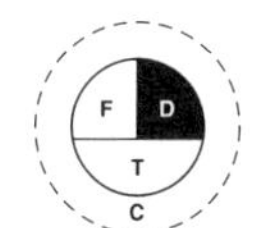

"CURRICULUM" SUGGESTS EDUCATION, WHILE A RED WINE STAIN CREATES A LETTER C FOR USE AS A BRAND SYMBOL. BUT IS THE NAME TOO SNOBBY?

"IN VINO VERITAS" MEANS THAT WINE LOOSENS THE TONGUE. USING ONLY "VERITAS" (LATIN FOR TRUTH), AVOIDS THE OVERUSED "VINO." BUT DOES IT SEEM TOO UPSCALE?

VERITAS

THREE OVERLAPPING GLASSES SUGGEST A WINE TASTING, BUT BOTH THE NAME AND THE GRAPHICS ARE MUCH TOO PREDICTABLE. IS THERE A WAY TO ZAG?

COMBINED WITH THESE GRAPHICS, "UNCORKED" SEEMS LIKE A FUN PLACE TO TALK AND TASTE WINE. BUT WHERE'S THE CONNECTION TO EDUCATION?

THIS IS A CLEVER REFERENCE TO THE FAMOUS INTERSECTION IN HOLLYWOOD WHERE PEOPLE LIKE TO MEET. BUT IS HOLLYWOOD APPROPRIATE?

"BIBLI" IS EUROPEAN SLANG FOR BIBLIOTEQUE, OR LIBRARY, WHICH PROVIDES A GOOD METAPHOR FOR EDUCATION. IT'S ALSO CATCHY AND BRIEF. BINGO!

Checkpoint 11: HOW DO YOU EXPLAIN YOURSELF?

All brand communications should emanate from an internal positioning line, or "trueline." A trueline is the one true thing you can say about your brand, based on your onliness statement. It must be something that your competitors can't claim (or won't), and something that your customers find both valuable and credible. Remember, it's not what YOU say, but what THEY say, that counts. In a nutshell, your trueline is your value proposition, the reason your brand matters to customers.

An example of a trueline is what people might say about Southwest Airlines: You can fly just about anywhere for less than it costs to drive. Or for Mini: The small car for people who want a fun driving experience. Or for eBay: The place to trade practically anything on Earth. From a customer's perspective, these are the basic, differentiating truths about these brands. They can't be reduced, refuted, or easily dismissed.

Once you have your trueline, it's a short step to a customer-facing tagline. For example, when Southwest says, "You're now free to move about the country," they're simply translating their trueline into a more polished form. What they're tapping into is our belief that Southwest offers a kind of freedom that we didn't have before. When Mini says, "Let's motor," they're translating a whole complex of feelings into a tribal message: If you appreciate small, high-performance cars like the ones found in Europe, and you hate the American trend toward clumsy, gas-guzzling SUVs, come and join us. And when eBay calls itself "the world's online marketplace," the company is reminding us that, as the planet's largest swap meet, it can offer the greatest number of buyers and sellers.

Of course, the key to crafting truelines and taglines is to focus on a single proposition. If you find yourself using commas or "ands" to write your tagline, you may need more focus. The rule? One proposition per brand.

Bibli's trueline grows directly from the thinking behind its name: It's the place where people meet to learn more about wine. But with a little polishing, and a slight shift in emphasis toward the customer, this trueline can easily be turned into a tagline: "Bibli. Educate your palate." Three words with no commas or "ands."

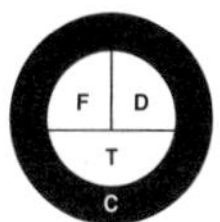

TRUELINES AND TAGLINES

1 A. G. Edwards takes a personal interest in your nest egg.
FULLY INVESTED IN OUR CLIENTS.

2 Citibank knows that money is only a means to happiness.
LIVE RICHLY.

3 Audi makes cars for people who take the road less traveled.
NEVER FOLLOW.

4 Chapstick is the secret to healthy lips in extreme weather.
MY LIPS ARE SEALED.

5 Bowflex equipment gives you gym-quality results at home.
WORK YOURSELF OUT.

6 Disneyland is the world's favorite amusement park.
THE HAPPIEST PLACE ON EARTH.

7 Charles Schwab is not just a company, but a real person.
TALK TO CHUCK.

8 Earthlink gives you services that make e-mail easier.
EARTHLINK REVOLVES AROUND YOU.

9 Nike helps you find your inner athlete.
JUST DO IT.

10 Heller Ehrmann is the legal firm that overturns the stereotype.
CHALLENGING THE LAWS OF CONVENTION.

11 Hooters is the politically incorrect restaurant for rowdy men.
DELIGHTFULLY TACKY YET UNREFINED.

12 Las Vegas is where the world goes to be naughty.
WHAT HAPPENS HERE, STAYS HERE.

13 Lending Tree rounds up online bids from lenders.
WHEN BANKS COMPETE, YOU WIN.

Checkpoint 12: HOW DO YOU SPREAD THE WORD?

Okay. So you've got a name, a trueline, and a tagline. Now you need to unpack the meaning hidden within those assets and deploy it across a series of touchpoints—the places where customers will come into contact with your brand—so they become true believers and spread the gospel to their friends. This brings you face to face with the hurdles discussed earlier—extreme market clutter, increasing demands on people's time, the fractured advertising model, and tribal buying habits. Where do you put your limited communication dollars to get the highest return?

Sim Wong Hoo, the CEO of Creative Technology, was quoted as saying, "Our biggest challenge is marketing. But I'm stingy. I don't want to waste money unless I know it's going to work." Apparently, Mr. Hoo believes marketing is wasteful even when it works. Contrast this attitude with that of Steve Jobs, CEO of Apple, who believes marketing is a crucial part of the product. Both companies sell MP3 music players, but Apple has sold more than 4 million per quarter, while Creative Technology has sold only a tiny fraction of that number since the very beginning. A recent tally puts the total number of MP3 models in the world at 14,659. How many brands can you name? The iPod?

In fact, a closer look at iPod's communications reveals very little waste. The same images that are used in TV advertising are also used on billboards, collateral pieces, trade shows, store environments, and retail packaging. The brand uses one voice across all touchpoints, the places where customers experience the brand. At the touchpoints where Apple marketers choose to compete, they win. Where they can't win, they don't compete.

While not every company can be Apple, every company can use Apple's approach to marketing. It starts with a zag, and continues by aligning all the customer experiences with the zag. Since a zag is designed to stand out from the clutter, a marketing plan based on zagging will appear much larger than it is. In the parlance of the day, it will maximize marcom ROI.

The Bibli budget, for example, could be focused on in-store communications so that customers become the channel for spreading the gospel. Touchpoints might include packaging, wine glasses, branded books and DVDs for sale, plus wine tips that customers can easily share.

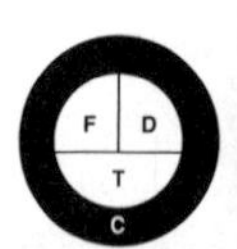

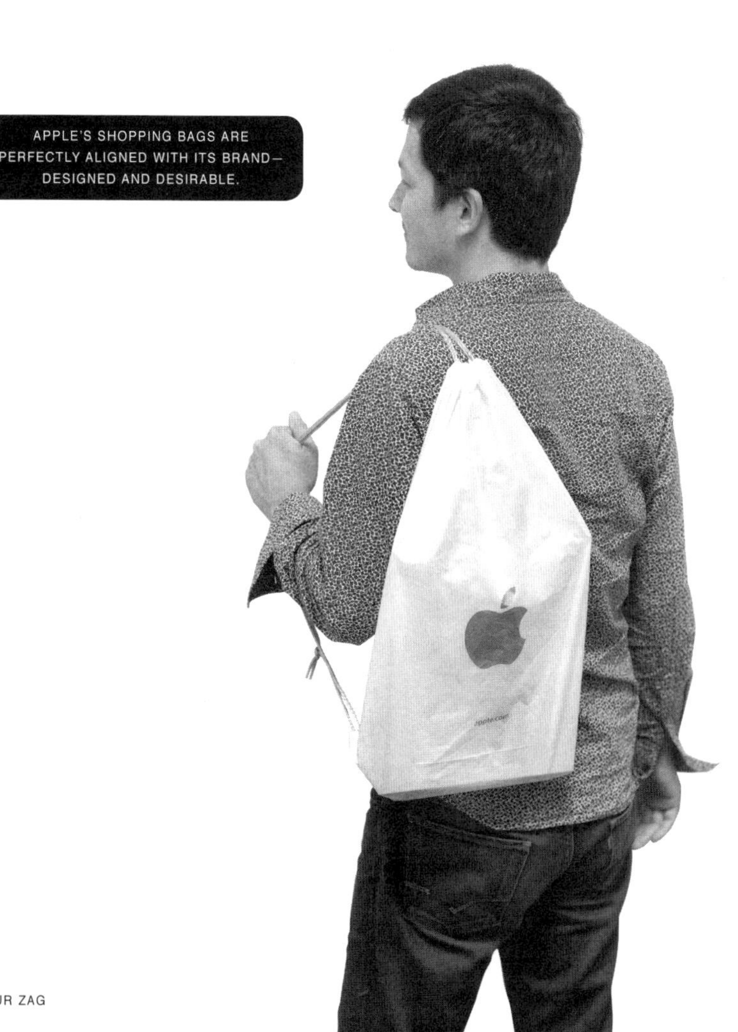

APPLE'S SHOPPING BAGS ARE PERFECTLY ALIGNED WITH ITS BRAND—DESIGNED AND DESIRABLE.

Checkpoint 13: HOW DO PEOPLE ENGAGE WITH YOU?

Before you can align your touchpoints, you have to define what you're selling and how you're going to sell it. Naturally, this has cost-benefit implications. But since a brand is a person's gut feeling, it's better to address the problem with gut feeling rather than cold logic. What you're looking for are ways to build your zag—later you can analyze the profit potential of the various components.

You may find that in building your zag you'll want to give away items that your competitors sell at a profit. Or you may find that your competitors are beating each other up by competing in the same way, or in the same areas, and that you can steal a march by ceding those battles.

In BLUE OCEAN STRATEGY, authors W. Chan Kim and Renee Mauborgne offer a systematic way to reposition competitors by changing the rules of engagement. The idea is to head for uncluttered market space (blue ocean) instead of space characterized by bloody competition (red ocean).

Since Bibli was conceived from the outset to occupy new market space, the founders might map it against the closest competitors, such as traditional wine bars, restaurants with wine lists, and wine shops with tasting rooms.

What can Bibli offer that competitors can't or won't? Inexpensive "learning wines" by the glass? Educational content presented on large video screens? Blind-tasting games in which customers compete to identify varietals? Group excursions to wine-producing countries? A content-rich Web site with a constantly changing tasting schedule? Demonstrations of food and wine pairings? Private-label take-home wines?

The best rule to follow when mapping your value proposition is to forget about so-called best practices. Best practices are usually common practices. And common practices will never add up to a zag, no matter how many of them you apply.

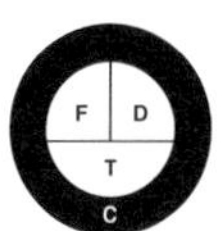

Checkpoint 14: WHAT DO THEY EXPERIENCE?

While strategy is a powerful discipline, many companies forget that without good execution a strategy is only a plan—an intention. Every year thousands of strategic plans fail because they weren't translated into compelling customer experiences. In short, the road to hell is paved with good strategy.

Customers experience your brand at specific touchpoints, so choosing what those touchpoints are, and influencing what happens there, is important work. The best way to start choosing and influencing your touchpoints is by mapping your customers' journey from awareness to brand loyalty. How will they learn about you? How can you help them "enroll" in your brand? Who—or what—will be your competition at each of the touchpoints? Where should you put your marketing resources? More to the point, where should you NOT put them?

The marketers for the wine bar, for example, might make a list of touchpoints that goes something like this: Word of mouth, driving by, walking by, introduced by a friend, newspaper ad, radio commercial, online ad, Web search, the Bibli

Web site, editorial coverage, direct mail, the design of the interior, the behavior of the staff, wine glasses, menus, product packaging, educational materials, on-site learning games, wine-tasting events, a wine travel program.

They might then prioritize them according to their potential for alignment. Thus, the interior space might be high on the list for funding, since it could be designed to encourage conversation. Electronics might also receive special attention, including a large video-screen array behind the bar, custom-designed content to deliver education, entertainment, and wine-tasting games, and ultra-fast checkout with handheld computers. Less important touchpoints would receive less funding, and others, especially those used heavily by competitors, would be dropped entirely.

Every brand is built with experiences, whether the brand is a company, a product, or a service, and whether it serves individuals or businesses. The key is to craft those experiences so they create delight for the people who determine the meaning and value of your brand—your customers.

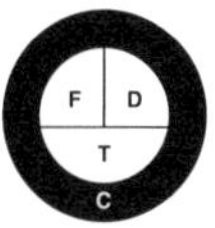

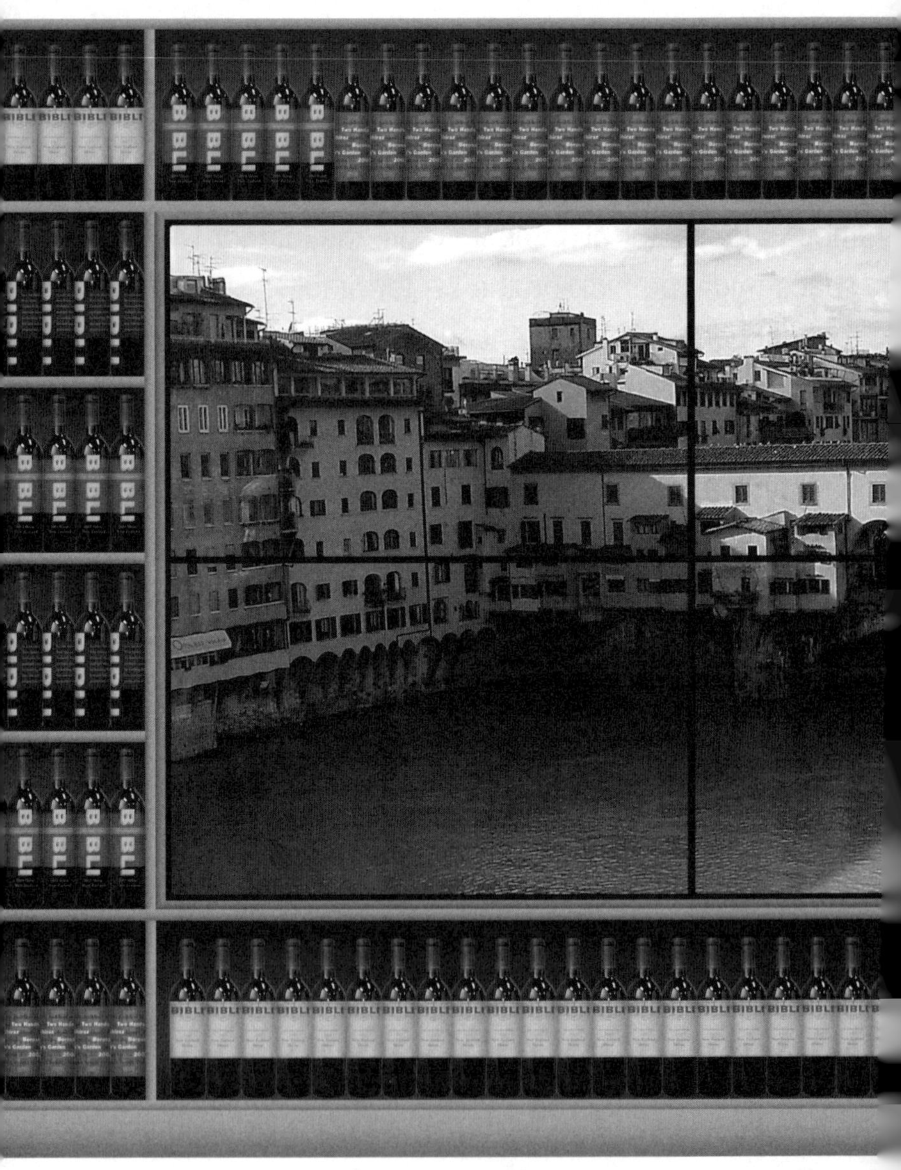

COULD BIBLI HAVE A BAR-LENGTH SCREEN SYSTEM TO DELIGHT CUSTOMERS

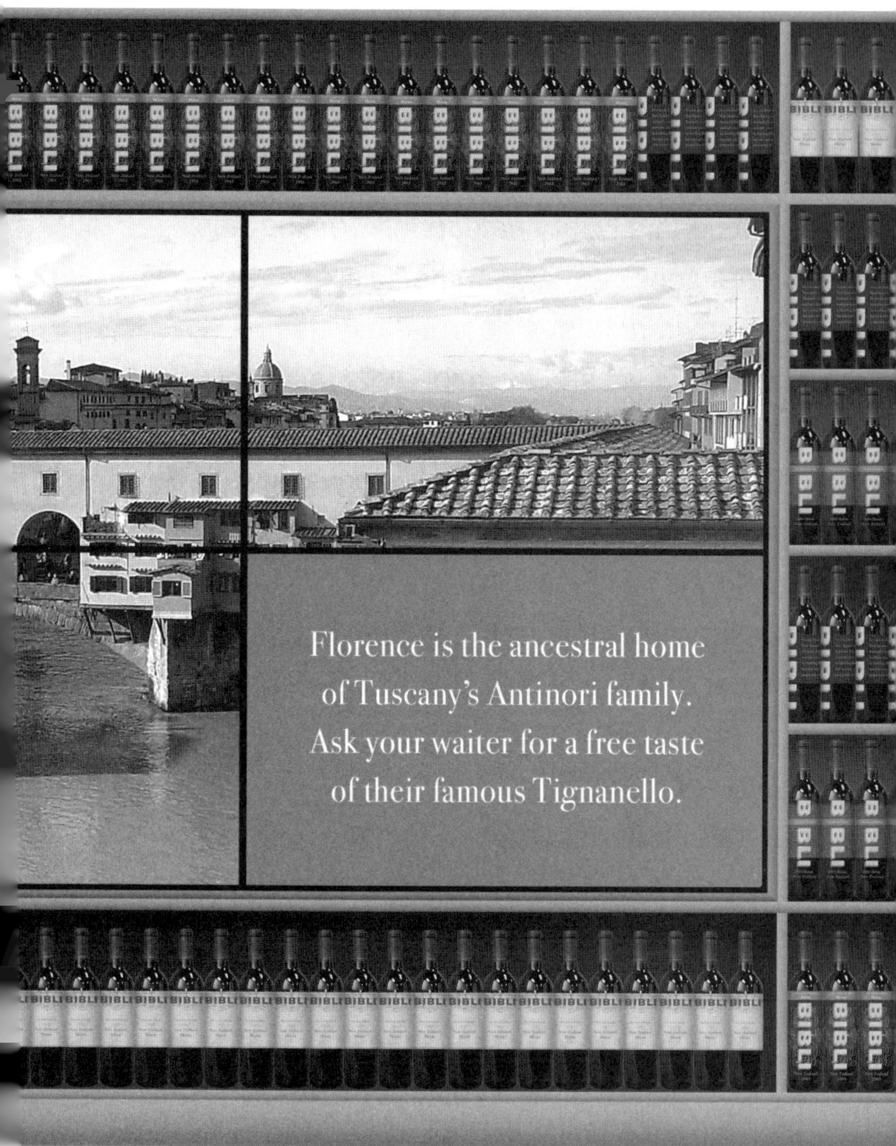
Florence is the ancestral home
of Tuscany's Antinori family.
Ask your waiter for a free taste
of their famous Tignanello.
BIBLI

WITH PRODUCT OFFERS, ENTERTAINMENT, AND LEARNING EXPERIENCES?

Checkpoint 15: HOW DO YOU EARN THEIR LOYALTY?

Let me toss some statistics at you. More than 50% of customers would pay a 20–25% premium for their favorite brand before switching to another brand. In some categories, a 5% increase in loyal customers can produce a 95% increase in profitability. In certain luxury categories, 10% of the customers generate 50% of the sales. It's enough to make any marketer's heart beat faster.

Scott M. Davis and Michael Dunn, in their book, BUILDING THE BRAND-DRIVEN BUSINESS, offer six reasons for encouraging customer loyalty: When customers are loyal, 1) they stop considering other brands, 2) they request your brand by name, 3) they recommend your brand to others, 4) they wait longer and travel farther to get your brand, 5) they accept brand extensions more readily, and 6) they continue to pay a premium price.

Here's another statistic. In today's cluttered marketplace, a full 80% of customers are vulnerable to competitive offers, and fewer than 20% are willing to recommend your brand to others. With the odds so steep and so much at stake, no wonder there are so many loyalty programs out there. Do they work? Most don't, and here are six reasons why: 1) loyalty programs are often based on discounts, which "train" existing customers to expect low prices and wait out normal prices, 2) they attract loyal customers who would happily pay a premium, 3) they discourage new customers by making them feel punished or excluded, 4) they encourage competitors to retaliate with me-too programs, 5) they reduce profit margins, which 6) reduces the company's ability to serve customers at formerly high levels.

The truth is, loyalty can't be programmed. As soon as customers begin to feel "stalked," they choose "fight" or "flight." They either figure out how to game the system, or else they run to another brand.

Maybe you've had this experience: A few months ago I popped into a Safeway to pick up some groceries on my way to the office. Normally I shop at another market, so I was surprised to find some very attractive prices. When I got to the counter, the checker asked: "Do you have a Safeway card?" She said if I wanted the low prices, I had to fill out an application. I abandoned the items on the counter, and haven't been back to a Safeway since.

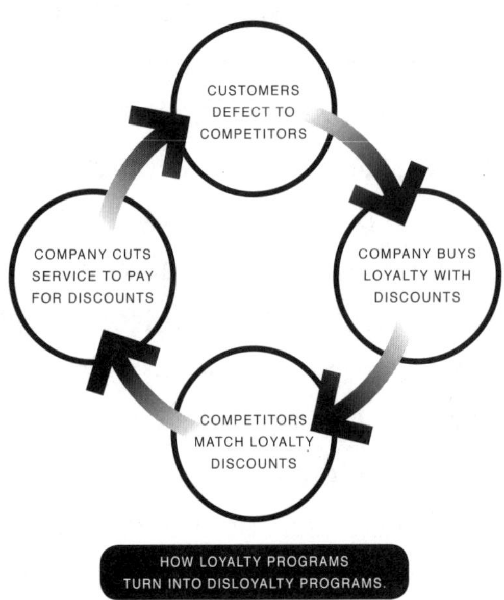

HOW LOYALTY PROGRAMS TURN INTO DISLOYALTY PROGRAMS.

Maybe you'd respond a different way. You might take the card, slip it into your wallet with your other cards, then play the stores against each other. In either case, where's the loyalty? It's missing, because real loyalty can't be bought; it can only be earned. It starts with companies being loyal to customers—not the other way around—and only becomes mutual when customers feel they've earned the loyalty they're receiving.

To illustrate the principle of mutual loyalty, let's imagine that one component of Bibli's wine-education process is a database that keeps records of the wines customers have tasted, along with their personal ratings. Customers could then access their history on the Bibli Website, either on their own handheld devices or ones carried by servers, to see what they've already tasted and get recommendations for other wines they might like.

As they get experience with various wines, a point system might automatically graduate them to higher levels of privilege. Maybe at "novice" levels they're offered a free taste of a premium wine with their next tasting flight. At "expert" levels they receive a discount on premium bottles of wine from the "library," which they can share with friends, introducing newbies to Bibli. Thus every visit to Bibli would become an investment in relationships, with the company making the first move, and customers reciprocating by bringing in their friends. With this model there would be no feelings of entrapment, and no sense of being punished for not being in the "program."

For brand loyalty to grow, it must be earned, and it must be mutual. As adman David Ogilvy famously observed, "Any damn fool can put on a deal, but it takes genius, faith, and perseverance to create a brand."

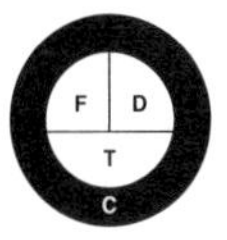

Checkpoint 16: HOW DO YOU EXTEND YOUR SUCCESS?

The thorniest question in brand strategy is how to keep growing. At some point in the life of a successful brand, marketers will feel the pressure to extend its success by "leveraging" the brand into other offerings. The hope is that the brand name will become a platform for a whole line of products or services, with each new product or service building on the customer loyalty already accrued.

Brand extensions can make a lot of sense. If the original brand has positive associations for customers, there may be untapped value that the company can mine. In return, new extensions can reinforce the meaning of the original brand, making it more valuable. Also, there may not be enough space in a given category to justify the resources it takes to launch and maintain a separate brand.

Extensions are often responses to internal questions such as: We have the customers, what else can we sell them (Virgin)? Or, we have the capabilities, what else can we make (GE)? Or, we have the brand, where else can we market it (Disney)? As soon as a company goes from a single offering to a line of offerings, it's in the brand-portfolio business.

There are two main models for organizing brand portfolios. The first is a "house of brands," meaning a company that markets a range of separate brand names. Here the individual brands are given the spotlight, while the company stays behind the scenes (Procter & Gamble). The second model is a "branded house," meaning that the company itself is the brand, and its products or services are subsets of the main brand (Hewlett-Packard).

The advantage of a house of brands is that each brand is free to fight its battles on its own terms, unfettered by the meaning of the parent brand. The disadvantage is that each brand must be funded, built, and managed separately.

The advantage of a branded house is that all the products and services can share the same budget, customers, and market position. The disadvantage is that all the offerings won't benefit equally from the company brand, and competitors will easily outmaneuver offerings that are saddled with strategically weak meanings.

HOUSE OF BRANDS

Either model can be highly effective, depending on the industry, the competitive situation, and the company vision. The least effective model is one that mixes the two models, leaving the portfolio stuck in the "muddy middle"—neither a house of brands nor a branded house—only to fade into obscurity as focused brands run off with customers. Both models require careful management, so that each brand and subbrand has a well-defined role to play in the overall lineup. "Looking at brands as stand-alone silos is a recipe for sub-optimiza-

tion and inefficiency," says David Aaker of Prophet. Read his book BRAND PORTFOLIO STRATEGY for a thorough treatment of the subject.

Back at Bibli, the founders are thinking ahead. If they manage to create a profitable business, how will they extend their success? By building a worldwide community of wine appreciation in which customers actively recruit more customers? By selling their private-label wines in stores? By taking the business model to other countries where people are curious about wine?

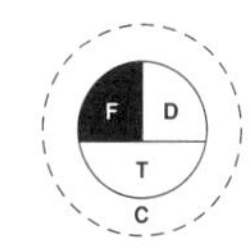

Checkpoint 17: HOW DO YOU PROTECT YOUR PORTFOLIO?

The era of the stand-alone brand is coming to a close, as more and more companies understand the value of linking brands together. While there's valuable synergy to be found in brand portfolios, however, they face four dangers that single brands don't—contagion, confusion, contradiction, and complexity.

CONTAGION, the first of the four, is the dark side of synergy. Just as customer loyalty can spread quickly through brand linkages, so can bad news. If one brand has a problem, depending on the strength of the ties between the brands, the rest of the portfolio can become infected. For example, a number of years ago 60 MINUTES aired a story on the Audi 5000's tendency toward "sudden acceleration," an untrue claim that spread like a forest fire through the media, the culture, and the courts. It ruined the reputation not only of the 5000, but of ALL the Audi models. It took years for Audi to restore luster to its brand.

By contrast, if the same fate were to befall Mini Cooper next year, its parent company BMW would suffer less damage. By building a separate brand for Mini, the company in effect has built a firewall between the two brands.

Thus, the choice between building a brand portfolio or stand-alone brand involves the trade-off between synergy and safety.

While CONFUSION isn't as dramatic as contagion, it's much more common. It happens when companies extend their brands past the boundaries their customers draw for them. I may love Crest toothpaste, but now that there are 17 varieties of Crest, I'm not sure what Crest means anymore. Rather than deal with my confusion, I may switch to Tom's Natural. At least I know what Tom stands for. Customers want choice, but they really want it AMONG brands, not WITHIN brands.

Brand confusion can be avoided by understanding the trade-off between stickiness and stretchiness. Stickiness is a brand's ability to own a distinct meaning in people's minds. Stretchiness is its ability to extend its meaning without breaking.

Crest
WHITENING EXPRESSIONS
EXTREME HERBAL MINT
SCRATCH 'N SNIFF
$4.19
$4.19
Crest
WHITENING PLUS SCOPE
Strengthens Enamel
Minty Fresh Striped
FLUORIDE ANTICAVITY TOOTHPASTE
$4.39
Crest
WHITENING PLUS SCOPE
WHITENS TEETH & FRESHENS BREATH
Cool Peppermint
$4.39
$4.19
Crest
MULTICARE WHITENING
Fresh Mint
EXTRA WHITENING
Clean Mint
$2.99
$4.19
Crest
TARTAR PROTECTION
Regular Paste
BAKING SODA & PEROXIDE WHITENING
Fresh Mint
$4.15
$3.29
Crest
CAVITY PROTECTION
Regular Paste
Cool Mint Gel
$3.29
Crest
WHITENING EXPRESSIONS
EXTREME HERBAL MINT
SCRATCH 'N SNIFF
$4.19
$4.19

For example, Dyson is closely identified with expensive, brightly colored, high-design vacuum cleaners. The brand has a high degree of stickiness in its subcategory. If Dyson were to add a line of expensive, brightly colored, high-design wristwatches, however, the brand could eventually forfeit its position in vacuum cleaners. Equally dangerous, if Dyson decided to stay with vacuum cleaners but market an inexpensive version alongside its original expensive version, the company would eventually find that its brand was defined by the low end, not the high end. The high end would then be vulnerable to a more focused competitor. Not only does stickiness limit stretchiness, but a downward stretch pulls perceived value down with it.

Of course, the temptation to stretch is nearly irresistible. Companies need to grow, and in the short term most brand extensions make money. In the long term, however, extensions can cripple a brand by confusing customers. Viewed through the lens of systems thinking, it would look like this: 1) the company needs revenue growth, 2) so it adds brand extensions, 3) which increase revenues in the short term, 4) but in the long term

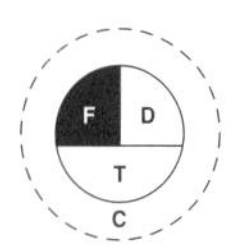

unfocus the brand, 5) which leads to decreased revenues, 6) which leads to a need for revenue growth, and around and down it goes. This is the brand-extension doom loop. The way to avoid it is through focus and long-term thinking.

CONTRADICTION can occur when a company tries to extend a brand globally. Since brands are defined by customers, not companies, customers in one culture may have a different view of a product or company than customers in another culture. The Disney brand, for example, may signify "wholesome entertainment" in one culture, "American entertainment" in another culture, and "cultural imperialism" in another. By extending its brand portfolio geographically, Disney risks cultural backlash from contradictory meanings.

One way to avoid contradiction is to build a separate brand for each culture, with a different name and a different set of associations for each. Another way is to focus a global brand on a common denominator. Hewlett-Packard's "Invent" position allowed it to travel easily around the world without contradiction or cultural backlash.

The last danger is COMPLEXITY. As a brand portfolio grows, what began as a way to simplify the brand-building process often ends up complicating it. Multiple segments, multiple products, multiple extensions, different competitive sets, and complex distribution channels can easily create an overgrown, hard-to-manage, inefficient brand portfolio. While the human mind is better at addition than subtraction, subtraction is the key to building strong portfolios—pruning back brands and subbrands that don't support your zag.

Managing a portfolio requires establishing clear roles, relationships, and boundaries for brands. It requires the sacrifice of lucrative revenue streams that unfocus the portfolio. And it requires a strong sense of what customers will allow the brand to be. "As provocative as it sounds," said CEO Helmut Panke of BMW, "the biggest task in brand-building is being able to say 'no.'"

Finally, the wine bar is ready to launch. The founders are confident about the clarity, direction, and market potential of their zag. While they still have many decisions to make, they now have a powerful decision-making tool to keep their brand aligned and their business profitable for many years to come.

Salud!

PART 3 : RENEWING YOUR ZAG

SCISSORS, PAPER, ROCK.

If you're launching a new brand, as in the wine bar example, you can stop reading here—you have enough information to start the zag-design process. But if you're repositioning a brand, or if you're curious about where to take your brand after you launch it, this section of the book will help you understand how and when to renew your zag as it moves through the three stages of the "competition cycle."

Whenever I give a workshop on brand positioning, I can count on getting this question: If focus is so important to success, how can so many unfocused companies grow so large? In other words, how can you explain the success of a company like General Electric, which markets everything from power plants to plastics, insurance to entertainment, and lightbulbs to light rail systems? Or Mitsubishi, which puts its name on 23,720 offerings from automobiles to aerospace, textiles to tobacco, and banks to broccoli?

The fact is, as powerful as the principle of focus is, companies with different degrees of focus can coexist in the marketplace. Perhaps the easiest way to understand how this can happen is through the children's game of scissors, paper, rock.

Remember how it goes? Scissors cuts paper, paper covers rock, rock breaks scissors. Each position has its strengths and each has its weaknesses, creating a balanced cycle of competition.

Business history suggests that companies thrive best when they settle into "stable states," conditions in which the business environment is fairly predictable and employees have confidence in what they're doing. In self-organization theory—the part of chaos theory that studies how order seems to arise spontaneously in complex systems—these stable states are called "attractors." As a company grows, it's attracted toward one of three main states, which we can call scissors, paper, and rock.

A "scissors" company is a startup or small business, often having only one brand. What distinguishes a scissors company is its extremely sharp focus. It competes by cutting out a small area of business (white space) from the market dominated by much larger "paper" companies, who are either too busy to notice or too slow to respond.

As a scissors company becomes successful and begins to grow, it morphs into a "rock" company, a medium-sized organization that typically has more brands and less focus. Its defining characteristic is no longer focus but momentum. Rock companies thrive by crushing “scissors” companies, who don’t have the resources to compete head to head with them.

As a rock company grows, its momentum begins to fade, and eventually it turns into a “paper” company. What distinguishes a paper company is its sheer size. With even more brands and even less focus, it survives by using its network and resources to smother “rock” companies.

And round and round they go.

There are three observations you can make about the competition cycle: 1) companies tend to grow clockwise, from scissors to rock to paper; 2) they tend to compete counter-clockwise—paper covers rock, rock breaks scissors, scissors cuts paper; and 3) the spaces between the stable states are “unstable states”—periods of time when change is not only possible but necessary. It’s during these unstable periods that companies often need to reposition their brands.

Now let’s look more closely at the ways each type of competitor can maximize its particular advantage.

GROWTH DIRECTION

COMPETING DIRECTION

THE FOCUS OF SCISSORS.

In the book THE INNOVATOR'S SOLUTION, Clayton Christensen and Michael Raynor divide innovation into two types—"sustaining" innovation, which calls for incremental improvements to existing offerings, and "disruptive" innovation, which attempts to find new market space, often with products or services that are less expensive and initially perceived as "not good enough." It's their focus on a disruptive innovation that allows scissors companies to outmaneuver paper companies.

So why don't paper companies counter-attack with disruptive offerings of their own? Because of "asymmetric motivation." When a company moves upmarket, much of the incremental revenue falls to the bottom line. When a company moves down-market, little of the incremental revenue falls to the bottom line. Large companies can't make enough profit on emerging markets, so they pass.

An example of disruptive innovation is eBay, a company that became "the world's online market-place" before the world thought it needed one. eBay thrived in the scissors state for the better part of a decade. Notes CEO Meg Whitman, "Young companies are very well served by focusing."

THE MOMENTUM OF ROCK.

As growth opportunities become clear, scissors companies move through the first unstable state on their road to rock. They may think about adding brands or subbrands, or acquiring other companies. Process begins to replace passion as they codify what worked in the early years. They may consider going public during this period, or bringing in professional managers.

When they do reach rock, they suddenly become dangerous to paper companies, who had paid little attention to them. The paper companies are now motivated to smother the rock companies by matching any new offerings—offerings that may be less disruptive and more like what the paper companies can profit from.

If scissors companies go public during the transition, their momentum may increase with the sudden infusion of cash, but it will soon be tempered by rising levels of risk aversion, as shareholders pressure management for ever-increasing earnings.

Yet rock companies have a tremendous natural advantage: The "big mo" allows them to enter new markets, attract world-class talent, and buy up the scissors companies they used to compete with.

THE SIZE OF PAPER.

Eventually, a rock company's momentum slows, and it passes through a second unstable state on its way to becoming paper. The biggest challenge the company faces during this transition is keeping the growth engine running. By now it has probably made some serious mistakes and may have lost a great deal of its original fire and focus. If the founder is still in charge, this will be the most likely time for a change of leadership.

The first thing the new leader must do is refocus the business and win back the confidence of shareholders. He or she will reduce head count, prune back unprofitable lines of business, and remodel the brand architecture. While the company will never regain the sharp focus of a scissors company, whatever it lacks in focus it makes up for in size. With size comes a broad network of customers, partners, distributors, and employees, plus access to large reservoirs of capital.

Just as scissors companies achieve the quickest success with disruptive innovation, paper companies tend to achieve it with "sustaining innovation." They win by making incrementally better products that can be sold for higher prices to attractive customers. Meanwhile, with rock companies breathing down their necks and scissors companies attacking them through the niches, paper companies are under constant pressure to grow even larger in self-defense.

There's strong evidence, however, to suggest that every company has its maximum size, beyond which it can't grow profitably. At that point it tends to renew itself by completing the cycle of competition—by fueling the next scissors generation. It refocuses, spinning off lines of business into smaller companies. It downsizes, scattering talented managers like seeds into niche businesses. And it discontinues investments in innovations that aren't likely to pay off big enough or soon enough. All of which refreshes the bottom line, and all of which feeds the success of scissors companies.

What can you do with paper-scissors-rock? Tons. Seeing where you fit in the competition cycle lets you 1) exploit your company's strengths and minimize its weaknesses; 2) exploit your competitors' weaknesses and better prepare for their attacks; 3) use the unstable states to reinvent your zag; and 4) renew your zag during the stable states to block a competitive move or simply remain vital.

HOW STRUCTURE BECOMES STRICTURE.

A business is a cultural organism. It grows and develops by creating processes and embracing values that formalize what generated past successes, so that employees can work more autonomously. These form the mental models, the organizational rules, that define a company's culture.

But when mental models go unquestioned, the culture stiffens. The company finds it increasingly difficult to react to challenges that don't fit its worldview. This is what Lou Gerstner found when he took over IBM in the 1990s: "Successful institutions almost always develop strong cultures that reinforce those elements that make the institution great. In fact, this becomes an enormous impediment to the institution's ability to adapt."

This "cultural lock-in" results in an inability to change, even in the face of clear market threats. When a company's capabilities reside in its people, changing to meet these threats is fairly simple. But when its capabilities reside in processes and values, lock-in happens and change becomes difficult. "The chains of habit," said Samuel Johnson, "are too weak to be felt until they are too strong to be broken."

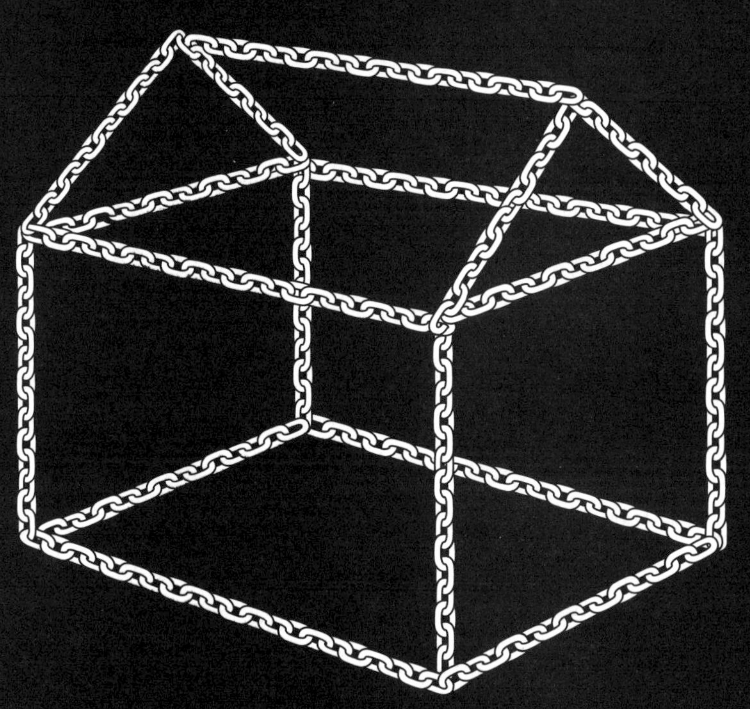

UNLOCKING YOUR ZAG.

Gerstner was successful in transforming IBM from a seller of "big iron" to a leader in technology services because he was able to address the central problem of brand-building: How do you get a complex organization to execute a simple idea? Of course, first you have to get a simple idea—a zag. Second, you have to use "generative learning" rather than "simple learning" to change the way the business operates. "Simple learning" is learning how to do the same thing better. "Generative learning" is learning how to do new things. "Most of all," said Gerstner, "it requires that the organization do something different, value something more than it has in the past, acquire skills it doesn't have."

Organizational theorist James March argues for an "influx of the naïve and ignorant" to jump-start generative learning. He warns that groups become progressively blind to opportunity when they spend too much time "exploiting" and too little time "exploring."

In the exploiting mode, groups focus on making money now by driving out variance and replicating the past. In the exploring mode, they focus on making money later and breaking from the past.

By recruiting fresh blood, a company can introduce people who have no allegiance to "the way we do things around here."

Mental models come in two flavors—those that make life easier by solving problems, and those that make life difficult by creating stuck situations.

The mental models of a mature organization will act like an elastic net—when you pull one piece out of position it will stay that way as long as you exert pressure. As soon as you let go, it will snap back in place. Yet change can be surprisingly easy when you identify the right place to achieve leverage. To find the leverage point in your organization, just ask these three questions:

1. What is stopping the change?
2. How is that a problem?
3. What would have to happen for it NOT to be a problem?

There's a myth that people in organizations don't like change. Actually, people do like change. What they don't like is BEING changed. When you find your zag, ask your people how they'll help to execute it. You'll be surprised by the amount of energy you release.

SIMPLE LEARNING
IS ABOUT DRAWING THE
SAME BOX BIGGER.

GENERATIVE LEARNING
IS ABOUT DRAWING A
WHOLE NEW SHAPE.

WHEN GOOD SHAREHOLDERS GO BAD.

At the Hudson Highland Center for High Performance, Susan Annunzio defines a high-performance company as one that makes money by developing new products, services, and markets. "The biggest impediment to high performance," she says, "is short-term focus." Short-term focus is often a reaction to the demands of shareholders, who are quick to sell off non-performing stocks. But non-performing stocks and non-performing companies are two different things.

The HARVARD BUSINESS REVIEW studied 275 companies over 11 years, dividing the companies into those that customers felt had become more differentiated and those that had become less differentiated. The more-differentiated companies realized a stock gain of 4.8% on the year; the less-differentiated companies a loss of 4.3%. Not only that, but the changes in stock price showed up ONE YEAR AFTER the changes in differentiation. In other words, customers saw right away what shareholders only saw after seeing the earnings.

Shareholders who are unaware of the relationship between zagging and performance are driving the bus from the back seat.

THE NEW PRIME DIRECTIVE.

CEOs are beginning to question the prime directive of creating shareholder value at the expense of other values. They've seen the slippery slope: 1) incremental investments don't produce fast growth, 2) shareholders devalue the stock, 3) the leaders are fired, 4) the new leaders cost-cut their way back to earlier earnings levels, and 5) the company is once again searching for fast growth.

Annunzio admonishes CEOs to "stand up to the investment community and tell them that companies can't cut their way to sustainable growth." Instead, "they should differentiate their products and seize opportunities in new markets."

Recent studies offer ammunition. Companies with 80% of their revenue from innovative products have typically doubled their market share in a five-year period. The top 20% of the most innovative companies have achieved double the shareholder returns of the 80% less innovative companies. And companies that have radically transformed their brands through differentiation have enjoyed tangible results, and stock prices have risen 250% a year as they've revived.

The new prime directive is zagging.

A TWO-STAGE ROCKET.

When cultural lock-in persists, a company may find itself in the same situation as Sears. Sears was once the leader in mail order, selling thousands of useful items through information-packed catalogs. To this day, many people believe that Sears is the best company for tools, appliances, and other practical products. Not satisfied with this position, however, Sears expanded from mail order sales to department stores, eventually asking customers to stretch their view of the brand to include insurance, a portrait studio, and "the softer side of Sears." Today the company is limping slowly toward oblivion.

Sears missed its big opportunity in the 1990s when it could have radically transformed itself by

THE OLD BUSINESS BEGINS TO LOSE ITS ORIGINAL MOMENTUM.

THE OLD BUSINESS DROPS AWAY AND THE NEW BUSINESS TAKES OFF.

returning to its mail-order roots, once again becoming America's most trusted store—online. Instead, that honor went to Amazon.

When a company needs to get itself from a dying market to an emerging one, the best vehicle may be a "two-stage rocket." Like launching a rocket, a new brand can use up half its fuel just escaping gravity. With this strategy, the company uses the first stage—its existing brand—to fuel the second stage—the new brand. By reducing investment in the old brand, and by selling off assets it no longer needs, the company can free up resources to launch the new brand.

Kodak has recently launched a two-stage rocket to complete its journey from the world of film images to the world of digital images. The company has halted its investment in film, and is now using the declining profits from the old cash cow to fund the new digital brand. It could have gone further by creating a new brand name for the digital company and reserving the Kodak name for use in the trade. A new brand name would have established the first major camera brand designed for the digital world from the ground up—a much more buzz-worthy zag.

ZAGGING AT THE SPEED OF CHANGE.

I began this book by citing Moore's Law, the 1965 prediction that computer speed would dramatically increase every year. I'd like to end it with "Warhol's Law," artist Andy Warhol's 1968 prediction that everyone will be famous for 15 minutes. Warhol's Law is based on the observation that mass media are becoming atomized, democratized, and personalized, not only allowing—but requiring—more people to feed the media machine. This phenomenon is inextricably linked with the big speedup, since constant change requires constant novelty. We're moving into an era of perpetual innovation.

As choices in the marketplace proliferate, the lifetime of a brand will shrink. Disk-drive pioneer Al Shugart was only half-joking when he said, "Sometimes I think we'll see the day when you introduce a product in the morning and announce the end of its life in the evening." The day is almost here. The journey from innovation to commodity is often so short that there's barely time to capitalize on it. What happens is that, while a company is betting its future on the success of its last product or service, other companies are busy launching the next product or service. Thus the market as a whole tends to move faster than any one company. In the big casino of the marketplace, the house usually wins.

So how can your company beat the house? Only by innovating at the speed of the market. To do this you'll need to shorten the span between invention and introduction. You'll need to launch white-space brands while core brands are still performing. You'll need to organize the company around brand collaboration. You'll need to beat marketplace clutter instead of adding to it. And you'll need to build a culture that thrives on radical differentiation.

According to a recent survey of CEOs, today's top three business goals are: 1) sustained and steady top-line growth, 2) speed, flexibility, and adaptability to change, and 3) customer loyalty and retention. Most of the CEOs said they'd be satisfied with any two of these. My advice? Be different. Go for all three with a brand that zags.

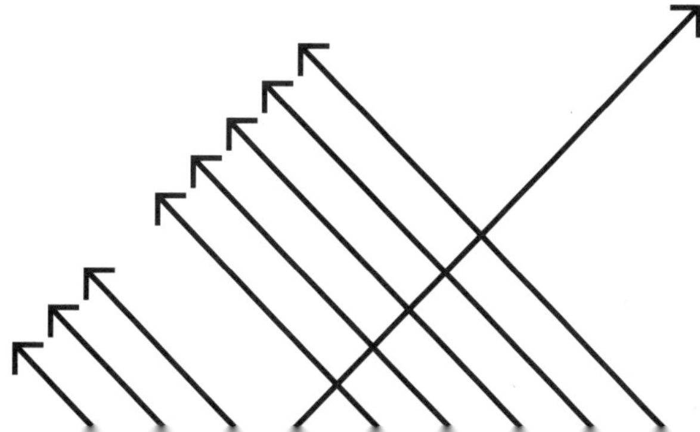

IF YOU'RE NOT **ZAGGING**

YOU'RE **LAGGING**.

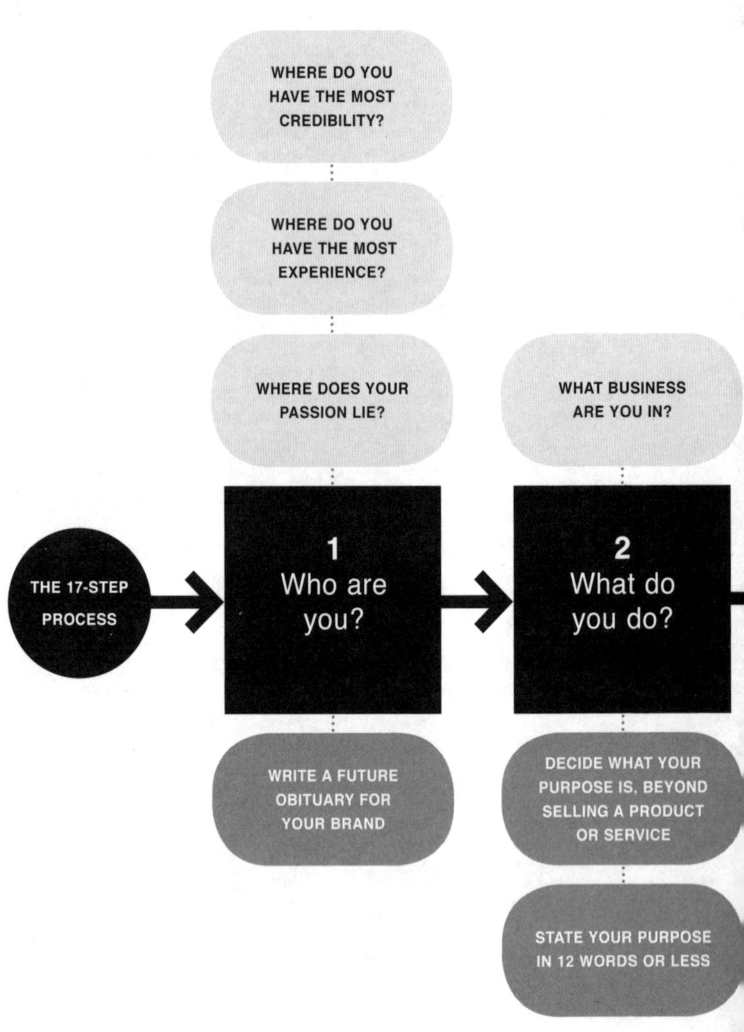
WHERE DO YOU HAVE THE MOST CREDIBILITY?
WHERE DO YOU HAVE THE MOST EXPERIENCE?
WHERE DOES YOUR PASSION LIE?
WHAT BUSINESS ARE YOU IN?
THE 17-STEP PROCESS
1
Who are you?
2
What do you do?
WRITE A FUTURE OBITUARY FOR YOUR BRAND
DECIDE WHAT YOUR PURPOSE IS, BEYOND SELLING A PRODUCT OR SERVICE
STATE YOUR PURPOSE IN 12 WORDS OR LESS

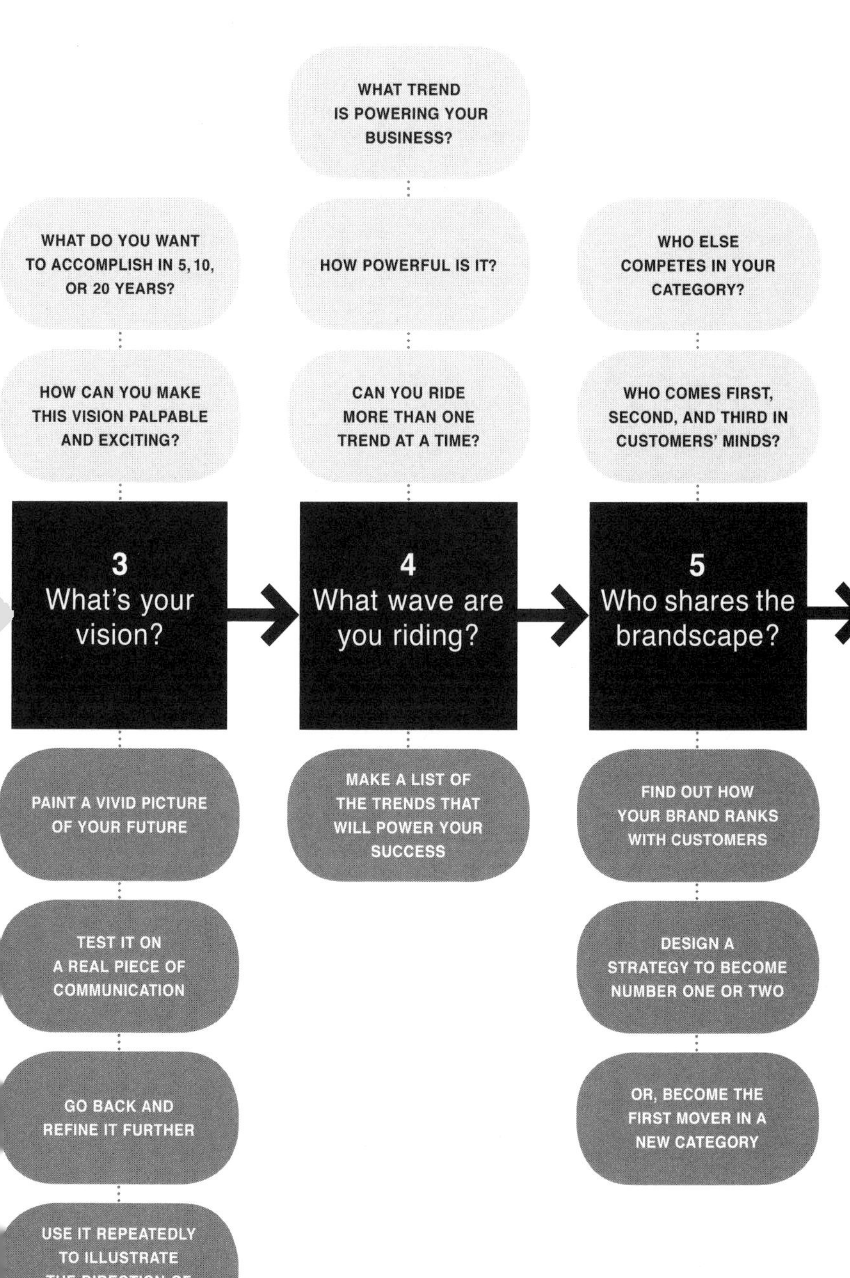
WHAT TREND IS POWERING YOUR BUSINESS?
WHAT DO YOU WANT TO ACCOMPLISH IN 5, 10, OR 20 YEARS?
HOW POWERFUL IS IT?
WHO ELSE COMPETES IN YOUR CATEGORY?
HOW CAN YOU MAKE THIS VISION PALPABLE AND EXCITING?
CAN YOU RIDE MORE THAN ONE TREND AT A TIME?
WHO COMES FIRST, SECOND, AND THIRD IN CUSTOMERS' MINDS?
3
What's your vision?
4
What wave are you riding?
5
Who shares the brandscape?
PAINT A VIVID PICTURE OF YOUR FUTURE
MAKE A LIST OF THE TRENDS THAT WILL POWER YOUR SUCCESS
FIND OUT HOW YOUR BRAND RANKS WITH CUSTOMERS
TEST IT ON A REAL PIECE OF COMMUNICATION
DESIGN A STRATEGY TO BECOME NUMBER ONE OR TWO
GO BACK AND REFINE IT FURTHER
OR, BECOME THE FIRST MOVER IN A NEW CATEGORY
USE IT REPEATEDLY TO ILLUSTRATE THE DIRECTION OF YOUR BUSINESS

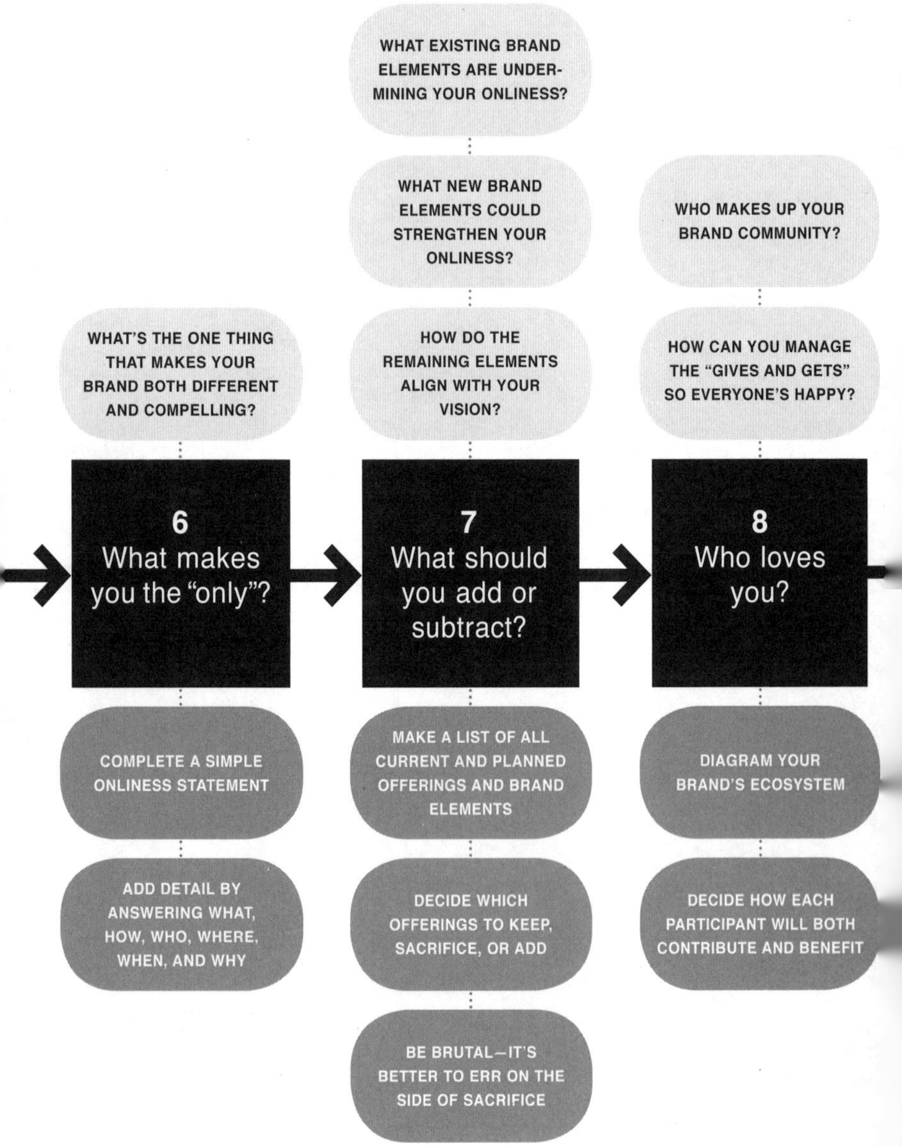

WHAT EXISTING BRAND ELEMENTS ARE UNDERMINING YOUR ONLINESS?

WHAT NEW BRAND ELEMENTS COULD STRENGTHEN YOUR ONLINESS?

WHO MAKES UP YOUR BRAND COMMUNITY?

WHAT'S THE ONE THING THAT MAKES YOUR BRAND BOTH DIFFERENT AND COMPELLING?

HOW DO THE REMAINING ELEMENTS ALIGN WITH YOUR VISION?

HOW CAN YOU MANAGE THE "GIVES AND GETS" SO EVERYONE'S HAPPY?

6
What makes you the "only"?

7
What should you add or subtract?

8
Who loves you?

COMPLETE A SIMPLE ONLINESS STATEMENT

MAKE A LIST OF ALL CURRENT AND PLANNED OFFERINGS AND BRAND ELEMENTS

DIAGRAM YOUR BRAND'S ECOSYSTEM

ADD DETAIL BY ANSWERING WHAT, HOW, WHO, WHERE, WHEN, AND WHY

DECIDE WHICH OFFERINGS TO KEEP, SACRIFICE, OR ADD

DECIDE HOW EACH PARTICIPANT WILL BOTH CONTRIBUTE AND BENEFIT

BE BRUTAL—IT'S BETTER TO ERR ON THE SIDE OF SACRIFICE

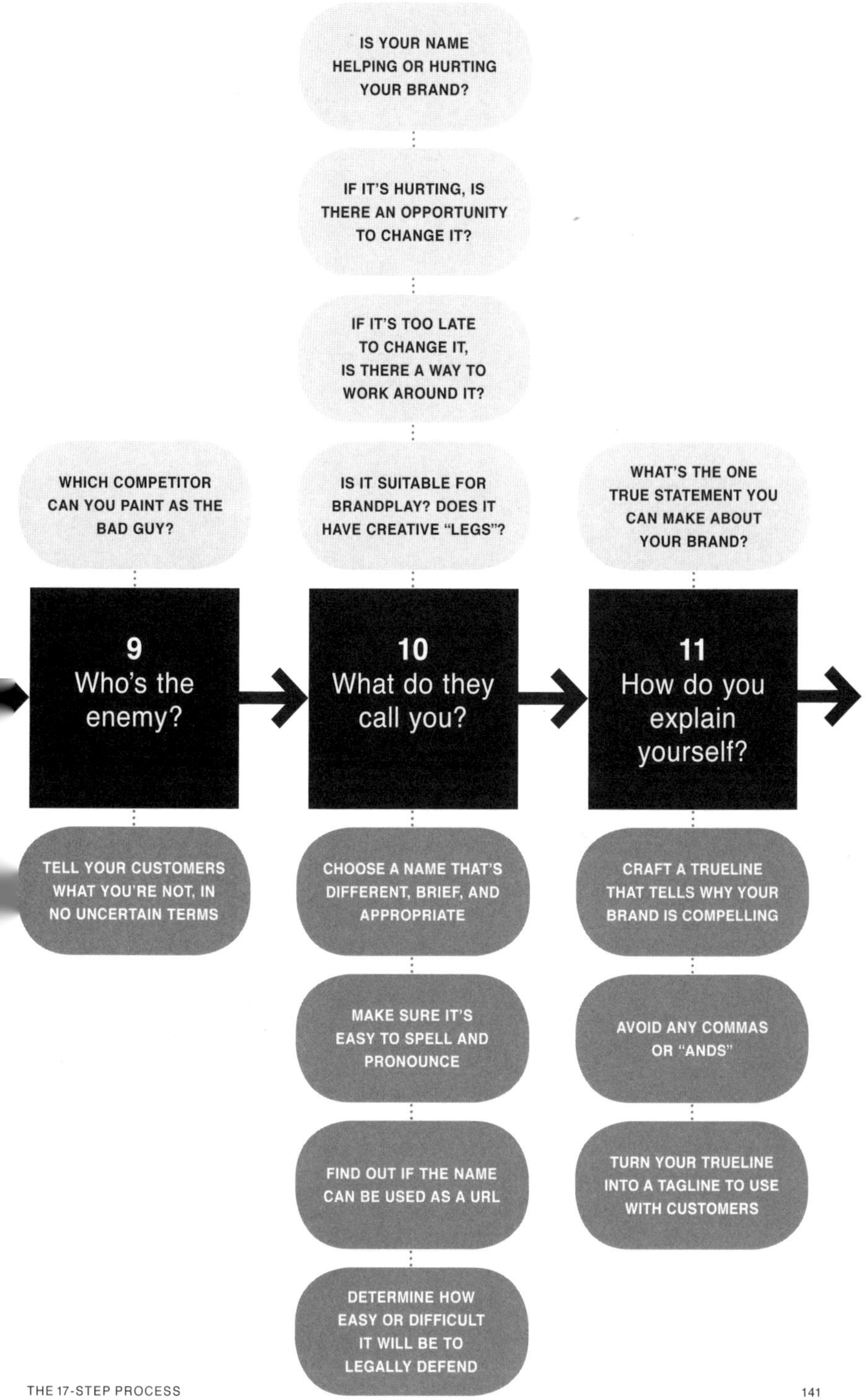

IS YOUR NAME HELPING OR HURTING YOUR BRAND?

IF IT'S HURTING, IS THERE AN OPPORTUNITY TO CHANGE IT?

IF IT'S TOO LATE TO CHANGE IT, IS THERE A WAY TO WORK AROUND IT?

WHICH COMPETITOR CAN YOU PAINT AS THE BAD GUY?

IS IT SUITABLE FOR BRANDPLAY? DOES IT HAVE CREATIVE "LEGS"?

WHAT'S THE ONE TRUE STATEMENT YOU CAN MAKE ABOUT YOUR BRAND?

9
Who's the enemy?

10
What do they call you?

11
How do you explain yourself?

TELL YOUR CUSTOMERS WHAT YOU'RE NOT, IN NO UNCERTAIN TERMS

CHOOSE A NAME THAT'S DIFFERENT, BRIEF, AND APPROPRIATE

MAKE SURE IT'S EASY TO SPELL AND PRONOUNCE

FIND OUT IF THE NAME CAN BE USED AS A URL

DETERMINE HOW EASY OR DIFFICULT IT WILL BE TO LEGALLY DEFEND

CRAFT A TRUELINE THAT TELLS WHY YOUR BRAND IS COMPELLING

AVOID ANY COMMAS OR "ANDS"

TURN YOUR TRUELINE INTO A TAGLINE TO USE WITH CUSTOMERS

HOW CAN YOU UNPACK YOUR NAME, TRUELINE, AND TAGLINE?

HOW CAN YOU ENROLL BRAND ADVOCATES THROUGH MESSAGING?

HOW CAN YOU ALIGN ALL YOUR COMMUNICATIONS WITH YOUR ZAG?

12 How do you spread the word?

MAKE SURE YOUR MESSAGING IS AS DIFFERENT AS YOUR BRAND

ONLY COMPETE AT THE TOUCHPOINTS WHERE YOU CAN WIN

WHAT ARE YOU SELLING AND HOW ARE YOU SELLING IT?

WHICH TOUCHPOINTS WILL LET YOU COMPETE IN WHITE SPACE?

13 How do people engage with you?

MAP YOUR VALUE PROPOSITION AGAINST THOSE OF YOUR COMPETITORS

SEE WHICH COMPETITIVE AREAS YOU CAN AVOID ENTIRELY

DISCOVER CUSTOMER TOUCHPOINTS WHERE YOU'LL BE UNOPPOSED

HOW WILL CUSTOMERS LEARN ABOUT YOU?

HOW CAN YOU "ENROLL" THEM IN YOUR BRAND?

WHO WILL BE YOUR COMPETITION AT EACH TOUCHPOINT?

WHERE SHOULD YOU PUT YOUR MARKETING RESOURCES?

14 What do they experience?

MAP THE CUSTOMER JOURNEY FROM NON-AWARENESS TO FULL ENROLLMENT

BET YOUR RESOURCES ON THE EXPERIENCES THAT ZAG

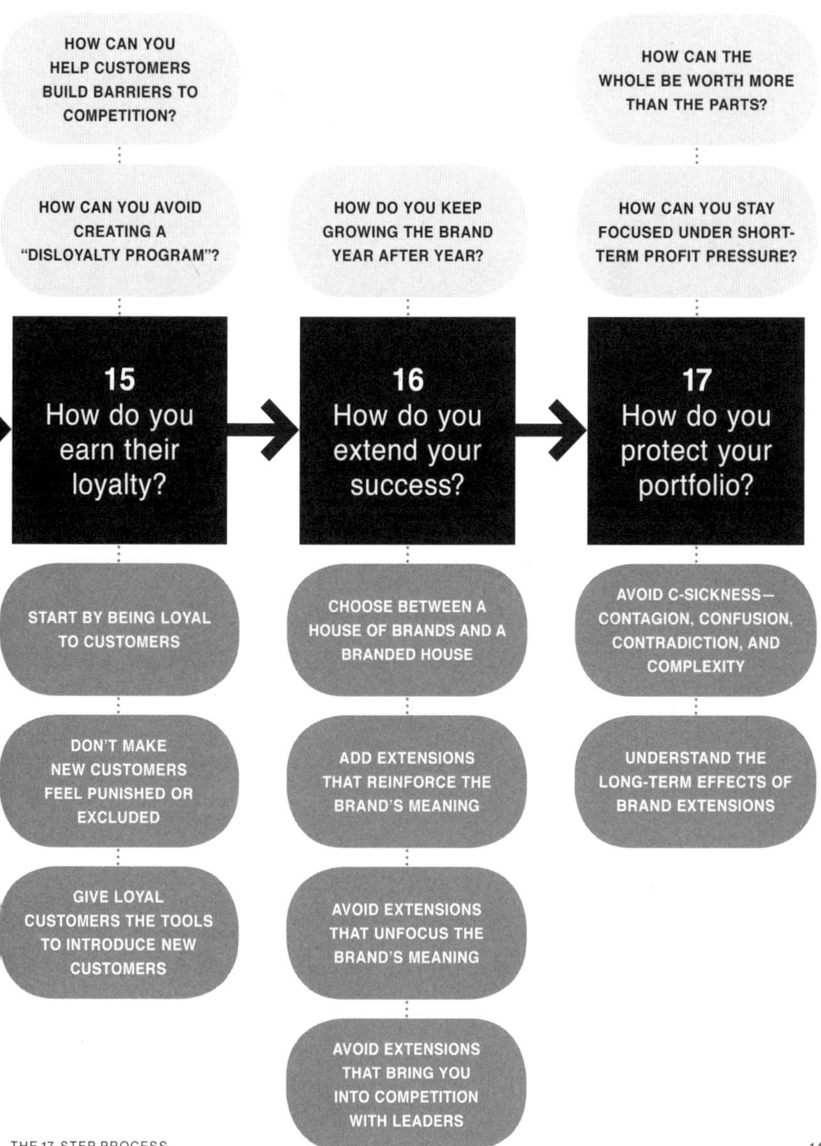
HOW CAN YOU HELP CUSTOMERS BUILD BARRIERS TO COMPETITION?
HOW CAN THE WHOLE BE WORTH MORE THAN THE PARTS?
HOW CAN YOU AVOID CREATING A "DISLOYALTY PROGRAM"?
HOW DO YOU KEEP GROWING THE BRAND YEAR AFTER YEAR?
HOW CAN YOU STAY FOCUSED UNDER SHORT-TERM PROFIT PRESSURE?
15 How do you earn their loyalty?
16 How do you extend your success?
17 How do you protect your portfolio?
START BY BEING LOYAL TO CUSTOMERS
CHOOSE BETWEEN A HOUSE OF BRANDS AND A BRANDED HOUSE
AVOID C-SICKNESS—CONTAGION, CONFUSION, CONTRADICTION, AND COMPLEXITY
DON'T MAKE NEW CUSTOMERS FEEL PUNISHED OR EXCLUDED
ADD EXTENSIONS THAT REINFORCE THE BRAND'S MEANING
UNDERSTAND THE LONG-TERM EFFECTS OF BRAND EXTENSIONS
GIVE LOYAL CUSTOMERS THE TOOLS TO INTRODUCE NEW CUSTOMERS
AVOID EXTENSIONS THAT UNFOCUS THE BRAND'S MEANING
AVOID EXTENSIONS THAT BRING YOU INTO COMPETITION WITH LEADERS

TAKE-HOME LESSONS

If you'd like a quick recap, here's a summary of the ideas covered in ZAG. Sprinkle liberally throughout your brand presentations, or try adding a different one to the bottom of each business e-mail you send—you may be surprised by the conversations you'll start.

MARKETPLACE CLUTTER

→ As the pace of business quickens and the number of brands multiplies, it's customers, not companies, who decide which brands live and which brands die.

→ Today's real competition doesn't come from other companies but from the extreme clutter of the marketplace.

→ Fighting clutter with more clutter is like trying to put out a fire with gasoline.

→ A brand is a customer's understanding about a product, service, or company. It's not what YOU say it is, but what THEY say it is.

→ An over-abundance of look-alike products and me-too services is forcing customers to search for something, anything, to help them separate the winners from the clutter.

→ The human mind deals with clutter the best way it can—by blocking most of it out. What's left, the stuff that seems most useful or interesting, gets labeled and stored in mental boxes.

→ For the first time in history, the barriers to competition are not controlled by companies, but by customers. The boxes they build in their minds are the boundaries of brands.

→ The goal of branding is simple: to delight customers so that MORE people buy MORE things for MORE years at a HIGHER price.

→ Customers today don't like to be sold—they like to buy, and they tend to buy in tribes.

→ In a marketplace of me-too offerings, people choose on the basis of tribal identity. "If I buy this product, what will that make me?"

→ The demise of traditional advertising has two causes: 1) People don't like one-way conversations, and 2) people don't trust advertisers.

→ What people want today are trustworthy brands. What they don't want is more intrusiveness, more empty claims, more clutter.

→ In a world of extreme clutter you need more than differentiation. You need RADICAL differentiation. The new rule: When everyone zigs, zag.

FINDING YOUR ZAG

→ To find a zag, look for ideas that combine the qualities of GOOD and DIFFERENT.

→ Artists are trained to see negative space. Companies need to think like artists when they're looking for new market space, because new market space, or "white space," is the secret to finding a zag.

→ When you're searching for a need state, don't think so much about the unbuilt product as about the unserved tribe. Look for a job people are trying to do, then help them do it.

DESIGNING YOUR ZAG

→ You need to clarify what business you're in—your core purpose. Core purpose is the fundamental reason your company exists beyond making money.

→ The leader's job is to shape and articulate the vision, making it palpable, memorable, inspiring. True vision leads to commitment rather than compliance, confidence rather than caution.

→ Without a clearly drawn vision, employees tend to work at cross-purposes, often taking refuge in functional silos instead of collaborating to transform a shared picture of the future into reality.

→ The power laws that control brand leadership can be reduced to a simple formula:
first mover + popularity = leadership.

→ When focus and differentiation are powered by a trend, the result is a charismatic brand that customers wouldn't trade for love nor money. It's the difference between paddling a surfboard and riding a wave.

→ While virtues like being innovative, responsive, and customer-focused are admirable, zagging requires that a company define itself by what makes it UNIQUE, not what makes it admirable.

→ Brands are subject to what network theorists call "power laws"—laws that explain why success attracts success, or why "the rich get richer."

→ In the world of power laws, market-share hierarchies are controlled by customers, who collectively determine the success order of competitors.

→ An "onliness" statement provides a framework for your zag: Our brand is the ONLY ________ that ________.

→ By checking any new business decision against your "onliness statement" you can quickly see whether it will help or hurt, focus or unfocus, purify or modify the meaning of your brand.

→ One of the most powerful principles in building a brand is focused alignment. The result of alignment is coherence; the result of non-alignment is wasted resources.

→ If adding an element to your brand brings you into competition with a stronger competitor, think twice. You may well end up wasting energy and confusing your customers.

→ A brand is part of an ecosystem in which each participant contributes and each participant gains.

→ Rather than trying to please everyone at the risk of pleasing no one, step right up and pick a fight. Just make sure you take on the biggest, most successful competitor you can find.

→ It's an ironic fact of marketing that a brand's most valuable asset is often the one given the least attention: its name. A poor name is a drag on the brand building process, and a good name accelerates it.

→ A name should be: 1) different than its competitors, 2) brief—four syllables or less, 3) appropriate, but not so descriptive that it sounds generic, 4) easy to spell, 5) satisfying to pronounce, 6) suitable for "brandplay," and 7) legally defensible.

→ All brand communications should emanate from a trueline. A trueline is the one true statement you can make about your brand. It's your value proposition, the reason your brand matters to customers. It can't be reduced, refuted, or easily dismissed.

→ The key to crafting a trueline is to focus on a single proposition. If you find yourself using commas or "ands" to write your trueline, you may need more focus.

→ A marketing budget based on zagging will appear much larger than it actually is. The object is to compete where you can win.

→ Forget about best practices. Best practices are usually common practices. And common practices will never add up to a zag, no matter how many of them you apply.

→ Without good execution, a strategy is only a plan—an intention. The road to hell is paved with good strategy.

→ Customers experience your brand at specific touchpoints, so choosing what those touchpoints are, and influencing what happens there, is important work.

→ Customer loyalty is not a program. It starts with companies being loyal to customers—not the other way around—and only becomes mutual when customers feel they've earned the loyalty they're receiving from the company.

→ If a brand has positive associations for customers, the company may be able to unlock value by extending it—but only if the new extensions reinforce the meaning of the original brand.

→ While there is valuable synergy to be found in brand portfolios, they face four dangers that single brands don't—contagion, confusion, contradiction, and complexity.

→ CONTAGION is the dark side of synergy. If one brand has a problem, the rest of the portfolio can become infected.

→ CONFUSION can happen when companies extend their brands past the boundaries their customers draw for them. Customers want choice, but they usually want it AMONG brands, not WITHIN brands.

→ CONTRADICTION can occur when a company tries to extend a brand globally. Customers in one culture may have a different view of a product or company than customers in another culture.

→ COMPLEXITY becomes a danger as a brand portfolio grows. What began as a way to simplify the brand-building process can easily end up complicating it.

→ The key to building strong portfolios is subtraction—pruning back brands and subbrands that don't support your zag.

RENEWING YOUR ZAG

→ As a company grows, it's attracted toward one of three "stable states," which we can call scissors, paper, and rock. Each state has its strengths and each has its weaknesses, creating a balanced cycle of competition.

→ A "scissors" company is a startup or small business that competes by cutting out a small area of business from a much larger "paper" company. Its defining characteristic is extreme focus.

→ A scissors company grows into a "rock" company that competes by crushing "scissors" companies. Its defining characteristic is momentum.

→ Eventually, a rock company expands into a "paper" company that uses its superior network and resources to smother "rock companies." Its defining characteristic is its size.

→ Focus beats size, size beats momentum, and momentum beats focus.

→ Companies tend to COMPETE counter-clockwise—paper covers rock, rock breaks scissors, scissors cuts paper.

→ Over time, focus grows into momentum, momentum broadens into size, size divides into focus... and the competition cycle begins again.

→ The spaces between the stable states are "unstable states"—periods when change is not only possible but necessary. This is the natural time to reinvent your zag.

→ Seeing where you fit in the competition cycle lets you 1) exploit your company's strengths and minimize its weaknesses; 2) exploit your competitors' weaknesses and better prepare for their attacks;

3) use the unstable states to reinvent your zag; and 4) reinvent your zag during the stable states to block a competitive move or simply remain vital.

→ There's a myth that people in organizations don't like change. Actually, people do like change. What they don't like is BEING changed.

→ To find the leverage point in your organization, just ask these three questions: 1) What is stopping the change? 2) How is that a problem? 3) What would have to happen for it NOT to be a problem?

→ The central problem of brand-building is getting a complex organization to execute a simple idea.

→ When you find your zag, ask your people how they'll help to execute it. You'll be surprised by the amount of energy you release.

→ The biggest impediment to high performance is short-term focus. Short-term focus is often a reaction to the demands of shareholders, who are quick to sell off non-performing stocks.

→ Companies that have radically transformed their brands through differentiation have enjoyed tangible results, and stock prices have risen 250% per year as they've revived.

→ When a company needs to get itself from a dying market to an emerging one, the best vehicle may be a "two-stage rocket." It can use the first stage—its existing brand—to fuel the second stage—the new brand.

→ "Warhol's Law" is inextricably linked with the big speedup, since constant change requires constant novelty. We're moving into an era of perpetual innovation.

→ The market as a whole tends to move faster than any one company. In the big casino of the marketplace, the house usually wins.

RECOMMENDED READING

BACKGROUND

THE BRAND GAP, Marty Neumeier (New Riders/AIGA, 2003). My first book on brand shows companies how to bridge the gap between business strategy and customer experience. It defines brand-building as a system that includes five disciplines: differentiation, collaboration, innovation, validation, and cultivation. Like **ZAG**, it's designed as a "whiteboard overview"—a two-hour read that can also serve as a reference tool. Look for the second edition, which includes all the definitions from **THE DICTIONARY OF BRAND**.

THE DICTIONARY OF BRAND, edited by Marty Neumeier (**AIGA**, 2004). This pocket-sized book is only available through Amazon. Published by AIGA, the professional association for design, it's the first book to "regularize" common brand terms. To get agreement on the definitions, I assembled an advisory council of ten thought leaders from the fields of management, advertising, market research, business publishing, and design.

FASTER, James Gleick (Vintage, 2000). This book is chock-full of facts that support something most of us understand intuitively—that the pace of life is speeding up. Gleick maintains that our era of "instant coffee, instant intimacy, instant replay, and instant gratification" is causing what doctors and sociologists call "hurry sickness." In **ZAG**, I didn't use copious case studies to support my point about the "big speedup," since Gleick has already done it here. Also, my readers are in too much of a hurry.

THE WORLD IS FLAT, Thomas L. Friedman (Farrar, Strauss and Giroux, 2005). As supply chains go global, the barriers between countries, cultures, haves, and have-nots begin to fall, causing the pace of business to speed up and the marketplace to fill with clutter and noise. This is no doomsday book, however—Friedman gives encouraging advice on how we can adapt.

THE PARADOX OF CHOICE, Barry Schwartz (HarperCollins, 2004). Conventional wisdom says that more choice is better. Only up to a point, says Schwartz, after which more becomes less. Choice overload can cause us to second-guess ourselves, adopt unrealistic expectations, and blame ourselves for any and every failure. Instead of empowering us, excessive choice can undermine us, leading in some cases to clinical depression. A good book to read if your goal is to reduce customer choice—marketplace clutter—instead of adding to it.

POSITIONING: THE BATTLE FOR YOUR MIND, Al Ries and Jack Trout (McGraw-Hill Trade, 2000). Positioning started as a brochure in the early 1970s, then grew into a book, and has been continuously updated without ever losing its salience. Ries and Trout pioneered the concept of positioning, the Big Bang of differentiation which soon they expanded into a dozen or more books, each viewing the subject from a different angle. If you can grasp the simple truths in this body of work, you'll understand what 90% of marketing people don't—it's the customer, stupid!

THE POWER OF SIMPLICITY, Jack Trout and Steve Rivkin (McGraw-Hill, 2000). Simplicity is always a hard sell, which is why it's so powerful in the commercial world. It goes far to explain the success of In-and-Out Burger, Google, the iPod, and Post-It Notes. It may also explain why the simplest advertising works best, and why ideas that take more that a few words to describe often fail in the marketplace. According to Trout, reducing complexity is the number-one way to streamline a business and maximize its profits. Simple, really.

THE WISDOM OF CROWDS, James Surowiecki (Doubleday, 2004). Surowiecki puts forward a fresh thesis—that large groups of people are smarter than an elite few, no matter how brilliant the few might be. This discovery is particularly useful in understanding why brands lead to customer "tribes." Customers know that if they simply follow the crowd, they won't go too far wrong.

FINDING YOUR ZAG

BLUE OCEAN STRATEGY, W. Chan Kim and Renee Mauborgne (Harvard Business School Press, 2005). A blue-ocean strategy is directly analogous to radical differentiation. It's aimed at discovering wide-open market space (blue ocean) instead of going head to head with entrenched competition (red ocean). The authors' tool for mapping a brand's "value curve" against those of competitors is especially useful for adding clarity and rigor to big-picture thinking.

DIFFERENTIATE OR DIE, Jack Trout and Steve Rivkin (John Wiley & Sons, 2000). Trout has never been one to pull punches, and with this book he and coauthor Rivkin give it to us between the eyes. For those who need copious examples and case studies before embarking on a zag, this and **FOCUS** (see page 166) are very good books. Did they say, "Or die?" Yow!

LEADING THE REVOLUTION, Gary Hamel (Plume, 2000). Hamel issues a call to arms for would-be revolutionaries, saying it's not enough to develop one or two innovative products—in the 21st century you need to create a state of perpetual innovation, not just with products but whole business models. Once an innovation becomes a best practice, he says, its potency is lost. "If it's not different, it's not strategic." Highly recommended for provocateurs on every rung of the corporate ladder.

PURPLE COW, Seth Godin (Portfolio, 2003). The author likens a differentiated brand to a purple cow. When driving through the countryside, the first brown cow gets your attention. After ten or twelve brown cows, not so much. Godin proves his point with innumerable examples from today's brandscape, and shows how any company can stand out from the herd. He also takes aim at advertising as usual, proclaiming the death of the TV-industrial complex. It's time to mooove on, folks.

SIX THINKING HATS, Edward de Bono (Little, Brown and Company, 1985). When executives try to brainstorm the future of their organization, the discussion can quickly turn to confusion and disagreement. Edward de Bono, acknowledged master of thinking skills, shows how to get the group's best ideas by focusing on one kind of thinking at a time. He organizes the session into a series of "hats," (red for emotions, black for devil's advocate, green for creativity) so that ideas aren't shot down before they're proposed. We at Neutron have used this system with our clients many times with gratifying results.

DESIGNING YOUR ZAG

THE ART OF INNOVATION, Tom Kelley et al (Currency/Doubleday, 2000). Kelley pulls back the curtain at IDEO to reveal the inner workings of today's premier industrial design firm. He shows how the firm uses brainstorming and prototyping to design such innovative products as the Palm V, children's "fat" toothbrushes, and wearable electronics. Cool stuff!

BUILDING THE BRAND-DRIVEN BUSINESS, Scott M. Davis and Michael Dunn (Jossey-Bass, 2002). It's all about controlling the touchpoints, those places where customers experience the brand. Davis and Dunn tell how to segment those experiences into pre-purchase, during-purchase, and post-purchase, so that everyone in the organization knows their role in building the brand.

BRAND PORTFOLIO STRATEGY, David A. Aaker (Free Press, 2004). David Aaker has spent more than a decade building a taxonomy of brand theory, helping to define and categorize all the dependencies needed for managing brands. Here he turns his attention from single brands to families of brands, showing how to stretch a brand without breaking it, and how to grow a business without unfocusing it.

DESIGNING BRAND IDENTITY, Alina Wheeler (John Wiley & Sons, 2003). A brand isn't truly differentiated until its personality is made visible through its identity materials. Wheeler's book presents winning examples of trademarks and other graphic communications, and offers a cogent description of how strategy and creativity meet in the real world among world-class companies. An indispensable reference tool that sets the bar where it should be—extremely high.

THE 11 IMMUTABLE LAWS OF INTERNET BRANDING, Al Ries and Laura Ries (HarperBusiness, 2000). While most people are still confused about how to build brands on the Web, the Rieses (father and daughter) log on with 11 new commandments. Daringly counter-intuitive, the book makes you question everything you know about the Internet.

EMOTIONAL BRANDING, Marc Gobe (Allworth Press, 2001). Creating emotion, aesthetics, and experience are the province of brand practitioners like Gobe, who uses his company's portfolio to illustrate and expand upon the work of David Aaker and Bernd Schmitt, showing how logic and magic are expressed in the practice of design.

EXPERIENTIAL MARKETING, Bernd H. Schmitt (Free Press, 1999). The age of "features-and-benefits" marketing is over, says the learned professor of marketing at Columbia Business School. He trots out a range of case studies to show how progressive companies are creating holistic experiences for customers, building their brands with sensory, social, and creative associations. Schmitt provides the academic underpinnings for any discussion of brand as experience.

MANAGING BRAND EQUITY, David A. Aaker (Free Press, 1991). Aaker fired the first salvo in the brand revolution by proving that names, symbols, and slogans are valuable—and measurable—strategic assets. If you'd like to begin absorbing the lore of brand building, this is the place to start. You'll learn why the words business and brand are becoming inseparable.

MARKETING AESTHETICS, Bernd H. Schmitt and Alex Simonson (Free Press, 1997). In this precursor to **EXPERIENTIAL MARKETING**, Schmitt and Simonson take Aaker's thesis one step further by showing that aesthetics is what drives emotion. What makes a brand irresistable? What styles and themes are needed for different contexts? What meanings do symbols convey? The answers to these questions are crucial in bridging the gap between business strategy and customer experience.

THE MISSION STATEMENT BOOK, Jeffrey Abrahams (Ten Speed Press, 1999). This is a handy reference tool, since it contains 301 corporate mission statements from some of America's best-known companies, including Johnson & Johnson, Kelly Services, TRW, and John Deere. The only time you'll need it is when you're working on a mission statement, at which point it will seem indispensable.

SELLING THE INVISIBLE, Harry Beckwith (Warner Books, 1997). A veteran of advertising, Beckwith takes on the toughest branding conundrum, how to market products that people can't see—otherwise known as services. His follow-up book, **THE INVISIBLE TOUCH** (2000), lays out the four keys of modern marketing: price, branding, packaging, and relationships. Those who sell tangible products would do well to master many of the same principles: If you can sell the invisible, the visible is a piece of cake. Both books are delightful and memorable.

A SMILE IN THE MIND, Beryl McAlhone and David Stuart (Phaidon, 1996). If you wanted to buy only one book on graphic design, this would be it. Designer Stuart and writer McAlhone prove that wit is the soul of innovation, using clever and often profound examples from American and European designers, plus a modest few pieces from Stuart's own firm, The Partners, in London.

THE TEN FACES OF INNOVATION, Tom Kelley (Doubleday, 2005). Kelley, from design mega-firm IDEO, maintains that the idea-killing power of the "devil's advocate" is so strong that it takes up to ten innovation protagonists to subdue him. He offers the "anthropologist," who goes into the field to see how customers really live; the "cross-pollinator," who connects ideas, people, and technology in new ways; and the "hurdler," who leaps tall obstacles that block innovation.

RENEWING YOUR ZAG

BRAND LEADERSHIP, David A. Aaker and Erich Joachimsthaler (Free Press, 2000). To be successful, says Aaker, branding must be led from the top. This shift from a tactical approach to a strategic approach requires an equal shift in organizational structure, systems, and culture. The authors prove their point with hundreds of examples from Virgin to Swatch and from Marriott to McDonald's.

BUILDING STRONG BRANDS, David A. Aaker (Free Press, 1995). In this follow-up to **MANAGING BRAND EQUITY**, Aaker acknowledges that many companies' brands are part of a larger system of intertwined and overlapping brands and sub-brands. He shows how to manage the "brand system" to achieve maximum clarity and synergy, how to adapt to a changing environment, and how to extend brand assets into new markets and products.

BUILT TO LAST, James C. Collins and Jerry I. Porras (1994, HarperBusiness Essentials). Brands may not last, but companies can, say Collins and Porras. The key to longevity is to preserve the core and stimulate progress. What's the core of your business? Your values? Your promise? This is the place where differentiation must start, whether your company is a house of brands or a branded house. The authors spent six years on research, which gives the book a certain gravitas.

THE CIRCLE OF INNOVATION, Tom Peters (Vintage, 1997). Co-author of **IN SEARCH OF EXCELLENCE** and author of **THE PURSUIT OF WOW**, Peters has discovered the power of innovation, which he calls a wildly unheralded business advantage. "Design is it!" says Peters. An example of innovative design itself, the book is a 10 on the Richter scale, guaranteed to shake the stuffing out of the stuffiest of stuffed shirts.

FOCUS, Al Ries (HarperBusiness, 1996). Ries (without Trout) argues cogently against misguided line extensions that dilute the strength of the brand. He shows how companies can evolve, increase market share, and grow shareholder value without undermining the focus that brought the original brand to the dance.

THE FIFTH DISCIPLINE, Peter M. Senge (Currency, 1994). Senge brought systems thinking—what he terms the fifth discipline—to the business management dialogue. Other disciplines include personal mastery and team learning. He encourages employees and managers to examine the mental models that at first allow organizations to codify their successes and later keep them from evolving with the market. Senge offers his own mental models, based on archetypal systems thinking, to help companies look at their businesses holistically.

THE INNOVATOR'S SOLUTION, Clayton M. Christensen and Michael E. Raynor (Harvard Business School Press, 2003). The authors show how innovative companies can disrupt incumbents with products and services that seem "not good enough" compared with those of competitors, while setting the table for future success. They also show that large companies don't have to sit idly by while scrappier upstarts reposition their business. A seminal work.

UNSTUCK, Keith Yamashita and Sandra Spataro, PhD (Portfolio, 2004). When all else fails, get **UNSTUCK**. This little book from a founder of Stone Yamashita Partners and a professor of organizational behavior is chock-full of tips and tricks for improving collaboration. The authors couple a highly visual communication style with bite-size ideas (a little like **ZAG**), to create a fun, easy tool for jumpstarting your team. More inspirational than instructional, it allows the reader to participate in the process.

ABOUT NEUTRON

Many of the ideas in **ZAG** come from my experience with Neutron, the branding think tank I founded in San Francisco in 2003. Neutron's mission is to help companies address the central problem of brand-building—how to get a complex organization to execute a simple idea. The field is bloodstained with brands that couldn't crack this problem.

Of course, executing a simple idea starts by **HAVING** a simple idea—one that's unique and compelling. Our experience has been that when a company's value proposition is simple, unique, and compelling—i.e., a zag—everything else becomes easier. Employees become more energetic, managers start to collaborate across silos, customers find reasons to become evangelists, other companies are more eager to partner, and shareholders give the leaders more headroom. These improvements, in turn, lead to market-speed innovation, stronger customer connections, and better operational efficiencies. Our role at Neutron is to make sure these improvements are predictable instead of accidental.

As you might expect, Neutron itself is a **ZAG**. We discovered new market space by imagining a role that didn't exist ten years ago: the job of "brand coach." As branding becomes more complex, companies are learning that it takes an interdisciplinary team to build a brand—not just one department or firm. Also, as branding becomes more critical to success, companies are feeling the pressure to manage their brands from the inside. Neutron has become the go-to firm for companies who believe brand management is too important to outsource.

How do we coach companies? Well, we're discovering new methods every day (since there's no prefab model for a **ZAG**), but we start by doing a lot of brainstorming in the areas of strategy and design (think-tank stuff). We develop new models (we call them conceptual toys) to help companies understand how they might drive positive change. And we develop the language, tools, and vehicles needed to deliver these ideas in ways the collaborative team can use (often within an educational framework).

If you've ever worked in a company where process overshadows purpose; where colleagues don't collaborate; where decisions seem disconnected; where brand expressions get lost in translation; where the spark of inspiration fizzles before it reaches your customer; or where it's just no fun to come to the office, you've experienced the uncomfortable gap between the spreadsheet-driven past and the brand-driven future. This is the gap that Neutron and our clients are working hard to close.

Find out more about Neutron at www.neutronllc.com.

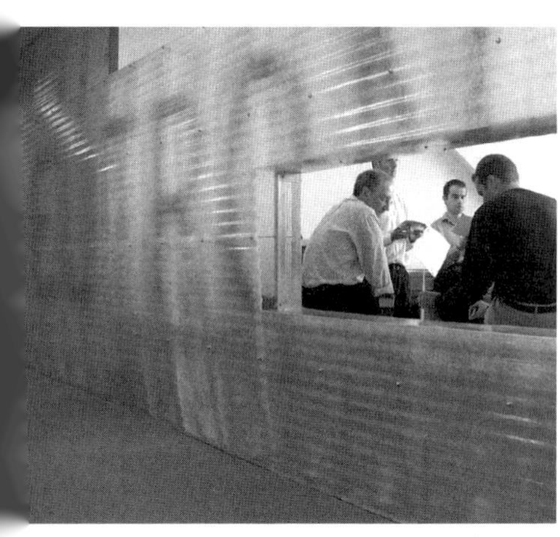

ACKNOWLEDGMENTS

Where do I start? Even though the book is brief, it took hundreds of people to bring it to fruition. At the front end there were many experts with whom I consulted about content, and at the back end there were many more who lent their skills to publishing, manufacturing, and marketing. In between, during the three years it took me to research, write, and design the book, I received guidance from many business thinkers who know their terrain much better than I.

Dr. James Forcier, for example, gave me his economist's-eye view of barriers to competition. Tim Calkins shared his "circumstances that favor the leading brand" and other insights from the brand strategy class he teaches at Northwestern University. Ron Sanchez, PhD, a professor at the Copenhagen Business School, clarified many strategic issues for me in his workshop on strategic management processes. And Gary Elliott, vice president of brand marketing at HP, helped me to think more deeply about the relationship between business strategy and brand building.

I'd like to thank my old advertising buddy, Garth de Cew, for the clever definition of branding that graces pages 24 and 25. Also my friend and former client, Peter Van Naarden, for helping me articulate the vision for Bibli—we got so excited that we nearly quit our day jobs to build a chain of wine bars. The wine bar vision wouldn't have been nearly as rich, however, without the previous input of hundreds of talented people who attended Neutron's branding workshops. Wonderful ideas.

Many thanks to my reviewers, including Brian Collins of Ogilvy & Mather, Jonathan Copulsky of Deloitte Consulting, Kip Knight of eBay, Rob Rodin of RDN Group, Rod Swanson of Electronic Arts, and Keith Yamashita of SY[P]. Thanks especially to Greg Galle of C2, whose relentless demand for a coherent story spurred me to work extra weeks tying together the loose threads in the narrative.

Also to my fellow authors for their warm support, including Al Ries, the go-to expert on positioning;

Seth Godin, the author of more fresh ideas about marketing than will fit on a shelf; and David Aaker, who showed the world why branding is more than identity, packaging, and advertising.

My sincerest thanks to Nancy Ruenzel and her publishing team at Peachpit, including Michael Nolan, who has championed my whiteboard overviews from day one, and the launch team—Sara Jane Todd, Scott Cowlin, David Van Ness, Brook Farling, and Charlene Will.

I couldn't have produced a single page without professional help. A crisp salute to my fellow Neutrons, including Deanna Lee, Josh Levine, Jennifer Murtell, Sue Smith, Laura Strojnowski, and Tonje Vetlesetter for their fine work. Hats off also to our Web team, Rob Bynder and Brad Benjamin, for cracking the problem of how to make a screen behave like a book (see www.zagbook.com). Finally, a huge hug for Heather McDonald, who took on the challenge of designing the interior pages with grace and good cheer.

I'm grateful for the use of Tim Baker's portrait in front of Guss Pickles, a New York institution since 1910. You can visit Tim, general manager, and CEO Andrew Liebowitz, a fourth-generation pickleman, at their newly expanded plant at 504A Central in Cedarhurst (left), New York, and order shipments online at www.gusspickle.com. Try their famous sour pickles—you'll instantly appreciate the value of specialization.

The actual writing of a book is a solitary activity, requiring that the writer spend long hours at the keyboard—mostly at night and on maddeningly sunny weekends—all the time fending off doubts of ever finishing. During the process it helps enormously to have a first-class support system. Therefore the lion's share of credit goes to my wife Eileen, for offering more patience, encouragement, and respect than any husband deserves.

Finally, love to Mom and Dad, my bookends, who have framed my life from left to right, top to bottom, beginning to end.

ABOUT THE AUTHOR

Marty Neumeier is Director of Transformation at Liquid Agency, a firm that develops programs to spur strategic innovation, build charismatic brands, and transform organizational culture.

Neumeier began his career as a designer, but soon added writing and strategy to his repertoire, working variously as an identity designer, art director, copywriter, journalist, package designer, magazine publisher, and brand consultant. By the mid-1990s he had developed hundreds of brand icons, retail packages, and other communications for companies such as Apple Computer, Adobe Systems, Netscape Communications, Eastman Kodak, and Hewlett-Packard.

In 1996 he launched CRITIQUE, the magazine of design thinking, which quickly became the leading forum for improving design effectiveness through critical analysis. In editing CRITIQUE, Neumeier joined the growing conversation about bridging the gap between business strategy and customer experience, which led directly to the formation of the management consulting firm Neutron and the ideas in his series of "whiteboard overview" books.

Neutron merged with Liquid Agency in 2009, creating a new firm that offers "inside-out" brand transformation services that include culture-change roadmaps and comprehensive brand marketing programs resulting in significant improvements in a company's ability to compete and grow through nonstop innovation. Liquid is headquartered in Silicon Valley, where innovation is a way of life.

Neumeier divides his time at Liquid among three activities—shaping client engagements, writing books and articles on business and design, and giving workshops on brand strategy and design thinking. Outside of work he enjoys cooking (badly), keeping up with movies (barely), reading (business), and traveling with his wife Eileen to destinations that promise romance and good food. You can reach him through the Liquid Agency website at www.liquidagency.com.